MW00967325

CHAMPIONS OF FAITH

Great Stories ^{VOLUME} 3 of the Bible

KINGS AND QUEENS

Merlin L. Neff

Pacific Press® Publishing Association
Nampa, Idaho
Oshawa, Ontario, Canada
www.pacificpress.com

Cover design by Gerald Lee Monks
Cover illustration by Clyde Provonsha
Inside design by Steve Lanto

Copyright © 2008 by Pacific Press® Publishing Association
Printed in the United States of America
All rights reserved

All Scriptures quoted are from The New King James Version, copyright © 1979, 1980, 1982, Thomas Nelson, Inc., Publishers.

Library of Congress Cataloging-in-Publication Data

Neff, Merlin L.
Kings and queens / Merlin L. Neff.
p. cm. — (Champions of faith ; v. 3)
ISBN 13: 978-0-8163-2266-4 (hardcover)
ISBN 10: 0-8163-2266-X (hardcover)
1. Jews—Kings and rulers—Biography—Juvenile literature.
2. Bible stories, English—O.T.—Juvenile literature. 3. Bible—
Biography—Juvenile literature.
I. Title.
BS579.K5N44 2008
221.9'505—dc22
2008007417

Additional copies of this book are available by calling toll-free 1-800-765-6955 or by visiting http://www.adventistbookcenter.com.

08 09 10 11 12 • 5 4 3 2 1

"Train up a child in the way he should go, and when he is old he will not depart from it."

—Proverbs 22:6

Interior Illustrations:

Robert Ayres: pages 21, 25, 85, 132.
Norman Brice: page 40.
Davis: page 33.
Ken Gunall: page 124.
Lars Justinen: page 60.
Joe Maniscalco: pages 13, 44, 48, 56, 65, 68, 84, 108, 128, 144.
Clyde Provonsha: pages 1, 81, 93.
John Steel: pages 8, 41, 45, 52, 61, 73, 76, 77, 89, 96, 105, 112, 117, 121, 136, 140, 148, 153.
Helen Torrey: page 100.

CONTENTS

FOR PARENTS

**Pass Your Values On to Your Children
Through Bible Stories**

As a parent, you likely want your nine- or ten- or eleven-year-old daughter or son to enter the teen years knowing the most important stories of the Bible. As you look for ways to pass on to your child the love of God and the principles that represent His character, consider how well a good story captures the attention of human beings of all ages. The Bible stories in these five volumes will place God's principles in your child's mind in such a way that they won't forget them as they grow older.

Read these books with your child—or have the child read the story to you—morning or evening or Sabbath afternoon, every week. This is a good way to build your child's character and faith in God without your having to explain a bunch of abstract ideas. Their awareness of how God works with His people will grow without them realizing it.

Every generation through history that forgot about the Scriptures, and therefore the knowledge and implementation of God's principles, has suffered greatly from its own evil and self-destructive actions. A similar destiny awaits the children of this generation if we fail to bring the stories of the Bible to bear on their lives. The stakes are too high, the dangers too close, for us to neglect the story of salvation as we raise our children.

The timeless truths of the Bible come through clearly in the stories of this five-volume set. Each story has been screened for some elements more suited to adult readers. The stories chosen are the ones that follow the thread of salvation down through the centuries. In places where people of the Bible speak to each other, the words are quoted from the New King James Version, which is fairly easy to understand and widely accepted.

Pray for your child that he or she will respond positively when the Holy Spirit speaks to his or her hearts. These Bible stories may bring your child to a turning point of knowing God in their own experience and accepting His love and His principles for themselves. There is supernatural power in the Word of God that may change your son or daughter forever.

The Publisher

"LONG LIVE THE KING!"

1 Samuel 8–12

Make us a king to judge us. Make us a king to judge us." The words of the leaders of Israel stayed in Samuel's mind long after the multitude had left the city of Ramah. The prophet had been a faithful judge over the people for many years, and now he was getting old. He had appointed his two sons to rule, but they often disobeyed God and treated the people unjustly. The people of Israel wished to be like the nations around them and have a king to lead them.

Samuel did not hurry to settle the matter, because he wanted the Lord to direct in the choice of a king. One day the prophet received a message from God: "Tomorrow about this time I will send you a man from the land of Benjamin, and you shall anoint him commander over My people Israel, that he may save My people from the hand of the Philistines."

Of course, Samuel was anxious to know whom the Lord had chosen to be king. The next morning he woke up early and went to the gate of the city to watch for the man who would be the first monarch of Israel.

A young man named Saul had been searching for some donkeys that had strayed from the farm of his father, Kish, a powerful and wealthy chief. For three days Saul and his servant had been hiking through the hill country, but they had not found the lost animals. The servant suggested that they stop at Ramah to seek the advice of the prophet, which Saul thought was a good idea.

GOD SAYS:

" 'Tomorrow about this time I will send you a man from the land of Benjamin, and you shall anoint him commander over My people Israel.' "
−1 Samuel 9:16

As the two men approached the city, they met some girls who were on their way to get water from the well. When Saul asked where he might find the man of God, the girls replied that the prophet was just then coming out of the city and that he was going to a religious service on the hill. Saul and his servant hurried on, and as they came through the city gate, Samuel saw them. When the prophet spotted the tall, handsome youth, the Lord said to him, "Here he is, the man of whom I spoke to you. This one shall reign over My people."

Saul, not knowing who Samuel was, approached the aging prophet and asked, "Please tell me, where is the seer's house?" A prophet was called a seer in Saul's time.

"I am the seer," Samuel replied. "Go up before me to the high place, for you shall eat with me today; and tomorrow I will let you go and will tell you all that is in your heart."

The bashful young man could hardly believe the words of Samuel. He had started from home to look for lost animals and never dreamed of going to a feast as a guest of the prophet.

"Am I not a Benjamite, of the smallest of the tribes of Israel," Saul said humbly, "and my family the least of all the families of the tribe of Benjamin? Why then do you speak like this to me?"

Samuel did not explain right then but led Saul and his servant up the hill. He brought them to a hall where there were about thirty guests, and he placed the young man at the head of the table. Samuel had directed the cook to save a special piece of meat for Saul, and when it was served, the prophet said, "Here it is, what was kept back. It was set apart for you."

After the feast, Saul went to Samuel's house, and the two men had a conversation up on the flat roof. Saul spent the night on the roof, which was considered a guest room.

At daybreak the next morning, the prophet called Saul to come down, and then he helped him prepare for the journey home. Samuel accompanied the young man beyond the city wall. After sending the servant on ahead, he took a flask of oil and poured it on Saul's head and kissed him. Then Samuel explained that the Lord had appointed him to rule over Israel. He also said that the lost animals had been found and returned to his father's farm.

Saul went on his way with a strange feeling in his heart. How was it possible, he must have wondered, that he had been anointed king of Israel? When Saul came near his home, his uncle asked him what the seer of Israel had said to him. Saul replied, "He told us plainly that the donkeys had been found."

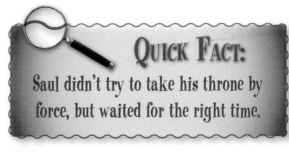

QUICK FACT:
Saul didn't try to take his throne by force, but waited for the right time.

The young man had decided earlier that he would keep his anointing a secret until the appropriate time to reveal it.

A short time later, Samuel called all the leaders and the people of Israel together at the town of Mizpah. The prophet asked the twelve tribes to walk by in front of him one by one, and under the Lord's direction the tribe of Benjamin was picked out. Then the families of the tribe of Benjamin passed by in review, and the family of Kish was chosen. Finally, a man of Kish's family was selected, and it was Saul. When the people close by called for Saul to come forward, he was no-where to be found. The Lord said to Samuel, "There he is, hidden among the equipment." Because Saul knew the outcome already, he had found a place to hide. When the young man was brought before the people, they saw that he was tall and strong. In fact, he stood head and shoulders above every-one else.

Samuel said to the multitude of people, "Do you see him whom the Lord has chosen, that there is no one like him among all the people?"

"Long live the king!" the Israelites shouted.

Samuel then described to them the behavior of royalty. He recorded the business of choosing a king in a book and laid it with the other books in the house of God. Then the prophet dismissed the crowd, and everyone set out for home. The Lord touched the hearts of some of the bravest men in Israel, and they immediately pledged their commitment to Saul. Others, however, were jealous and despised the new king. They whispered among themselves, "How can this man save us?"

Saul went home and returned to work on the family farm. Meanwhile, across the Jordan River, the savage people of Ammon threatened the Israelite inhabitants of Jabesh Gilead. Nahash, the ruthless Ammonite king, declared that he would make peace with the city on only one condition. "On this condition I will make a covenant with you," he said, "that I may put out all your right eyes, and bring reproach on all Israel."

"Hold off for seven days, that we may send messengers to all the territory of Israel," the leaders of Jabesh responded. "And then, if there is no one to save us, we will come out to you." Then they sent messengers to Saul's hometown of Gibeah, calling for help. When Saul heard the terrible news, he killed a pair of oxen, cut the bodies into pieces, and sent a piece to each of the tribes of Israel with messengers who said,

"Whoever does not go out with Saul and Samuel to battle, so it shall be done to his oxen."

The people rallied quickly, and 330,000 men met Saul at Bezek. The messengers from Jabesh prepared to return to their city after Saul instructed them, "Thus you shall say to the men of Jabesh Gilead: 'Tomorrow, by the time the sun is hot, you shall have help.' " First dividing his warriors into three companies, Saul then marched them eastward until they crossed the Jordan River and faced the enemy. From morning until midday the armies fought, and the Ammonite soldiers were either killed or scattered.

As the Israelite warriors celebrated their victory, some of them remembered the words of those who had despised Saul. They hurried to Samuel and said, "Who is he who said, 'Shall Saul reign over us?' Bring the men, that we may put them to death."

THOUGHT QUESTION:

Why didn't Saul want the men who opposed him to be put to death?

But Saul overheard them and said, "Not a man shall be put to death this day, for today the Lord has accomplished salvation in Israel." Instead of taking the glory himself, Saul gave God all the credit for the victory over the Ammonites.

Samuel, who had witnessed the battle, called the people together and said, "Come, let us go to Gilgal and renew the kingdom there." Gilgal was the historic town by the Jordan where the children of Israel made their first camp after entering the land of Canaan. There they made Saul king of the nation of Israel. They made sacrifices of peace offerings before the Lord, and Saul and all the men of Israel celebrated with great happiness.

Samuel stood up to address the people. He said, "Indeed I have heeded your voice in all that you said to me, and have made a king over you. And now here is the king, walking before you; and I am old and grayheaded, and look, my sons are with you. I have walked before you from my childhood to this day." The prophet then asked them if he had ever cheated anyone or judged them unfairly. The people said a resounding No. He told them, "Now therefore, here is the king whom you have chosen and whom you have desired. And take note, [it is] the Lord [who] has set a king over you. If you fear the Lord and serve Him and obey His voice, and do not rebel against the commandment of the Lord, then both you and the king who reigns over you will continue following the Lord your God. However, if you do not obey the voice of the Lord, but rebel against the commandment of the Lord, then the hand of the Lord will be against you, as it was against your fathers."

Finally, the old prophet presented Israel with a challenge. "Is today not the wheat harvest? I will call to the Lord, and He will send thunder and rain, that you may perceive and see that your wickedness is great, which you have done in the sight of the Lord, in asking a king for yourselves."

That day, God sent rain and thunder, and the people feared both God and Samuel. "Pray for your servants to the Lord your God," the Israelites said, "that we may not die; for we have added to all our sins the evil of asking a king for ourselves."

"Do not fear," Samuel replied. "You have done all this wickedness; yet do not turn aside from following the Lord, but serve the Lord with all your heart; . . . for consider what great things He has done for you."

THE DISOBEDIENT KING

1 Samuel 13–15

At the time of his first victory, King Saul should have led his large army against the other enemies that threatened Israel, so that he might give freedom to all his people. Instead, the king disbanded the main body of his army, keeping only two thousand soldiers with him at Michmash. He placed another thousand warriors under the command of his son, Jonathan, at Gibeah.

The Israelites had been severely oppressed by the Philistines during the many years of the judges. The enemy had taken all the swords and spears from the men of Israel and had left no metal workers in the country to make weapons. The Israelite farmers were forced to go to the land of the Philistines whenever they needed to sharpen their plows and sickles. Without swords, the soldiers of King Saul were at a great disadvantage in battle. In spite of this sad plight, the king made no effort to arm his men properly, and they were forced to fight with bows, slings, axes, and mattocks.

In the second year of Saul's reign, Jonathan grew impatient because his father would not attack the enemy. The arrogant

Philistines came with thousands of chariots, horsemen, and soldiers, challenging the men of Israel to fight. Some warriors of Saul's army acted cowardly; they slipped away from the camp and hid in caves and among the rocks of the hills. When Jonathan saw the Philistines encamped at Michmash, a rocky hill across the valley from the crags where the Israelites were hiding, he went into action. Trusting in the power of God to help him, he said to the faithful young man who carried his armor, "Come, let us go over to the Philistines' garrison that is on the other side."

Without telling anyone else of his plan, Jonathan and his armorbearer made their way down the mountainside, across the valley, and up the steep cliffs to where the Philistine fortress stood. When the enemy guards saw the two soldiers from Israel climbing up the rocks, they said, "Look, the Hebrews are coming out of the holes where they have hidden." The

God Says:

" 'For nothing restrains the Lord from saving by many or by few.' "
–1 Samuel 14:6

guards mocked Jonathan and his armorbearer, calling out, "Come up to us, and we will show you something."

Jonathan accepted the challenge as a sign that God was with him. He and his armorbearer moved out of sight of the Philistines and made their way on hands and knees along a steep and difficult path. Suddenly they reached the summit, overpowered the guards, and killed about twenty Philistines.

Terror took hold of the enemy forces, and, to make matters worse for them, an earthquake shook the mountain. The Philistine soldiers panicked and began to retreat. When King Saul heard the noise and saw the enemy army disappearing, he commanded his men to attack. Many of the Israelite soldiers who had deserted came out of hiding and joined in the battle. Soon the Philistines were routed and driven back to their own country.

After this, Saul chose the bravest men he could find for his army, and he appointed his cousin, Abner, to be his general. In successive battles he defeated the armies of Moab, Ammon, and Edom. But there was another enemy that had long troubled Israel, the Amalekites. When Samuel saw how successful the king was in battle, he sent Saul a message commanding him to make war against this wicked nation. The aged prophet reminded the king of the vicious attack the tribe of Amalek had made on the children of Israel when Moses was leading the people through the desert. God had promised that this nation would someday be destroyed for its terrible deeds. Samuel believed that the time had arrived for the enemy to be vanquished. The prophet said to Saul, "The Lord sent me to anoint you king over His people, over Israel. Now therefore, heed the voice of the words of the Lord. Thus says the Lord of hosts: 'I will punish Amalek for what he did to Israel, how he ambushed him on the way when he came up from Egypt. Now go and attack Amalek, and utterly destroy all that they have, and do not spare them. But kill both man and woman, infant and nursing child, ox and sheep, camel and donkey.' "

With an army of 210,000 men, Saul marched against the Amalekites. In a brilliant victory he destroyed most of the

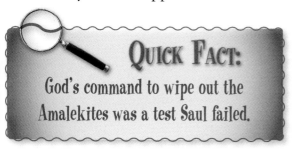

Quick Fact:

God's command to wipe out the Amalekites was a test Saul failed.

tribe. But he spared Agag the king, and he allowed the soldiers of Israel to keep the best of the sheep, lambs, oxen, and calves. Selfish King Saul decided to keep this booty in spite of God's command to destroy everything.

Early in the morning Samuel met Saul and his army at Gilgal. The king said proudly to the prophet, "Blessed are you of the Lord! I have performed the commandment of the Lord."

"What then is this bleating of the sheep in my ears, and the lowing of the oxen which I hear?" asked Samuel.

Saul attempted to excuse himself and blame his soldiers for his own disobedience. "They have brought them from the Amalekites," said Saul, "for the people spared the best of the sheep and the oxen, to sacrifice to the Lord your God; and the rest we have utterly destroyed."

"Be quiet! And I will tell you what the Lord said to me last night," said Samuel to Saul. "Did not the Lord anoint you king over Israel? Now the Lord sent you on a mission, and said, 'Go, and utterly destroy the sinners, the Amalekites, and fight against them until they are consumed.' Why then did you not obey the voice of the Lord? Why did you swoop down on the spoil, and do evil in the sight of the Lord?"

"But I have obeyed the voice of the Lord," Saul insisted, "and gone on the mission on which the Lord sent me, and brought back Agag king of Amalek; I have utterly destroyed the Amalekites."

But Samuel answered,

> "Has the Lord as great delight in burnt offerings
> and sacrifices,
> As in obeying the voice of the Lord?
> Behold, to obey is better than sacrifice,
> And to heed than the fat of rams.

For rebellion is as the sin of witchcraft,
And stubbornness is as iniquity and idolatry.
Because you have rejected the word of the Lord,
He also has rejected you from being king."

Then Saul said, "I have sinned, for I have transgressed the commandment of the Lord and your words, because I feared the people and obeyed their voice. Now therefore, please pardon my sin, and return with me, that I may worship the Lord."

Samuel replied, "I will not return with you, for you have rejected the word of the Lord, and the Lord has rejected you from being king over Israel." Then the faithful old prophet sent for Agag, the cruel king of the Amalekites, whom Saul had spared. Samuel took a sword and killed Agag before the Lord in Gilgal.

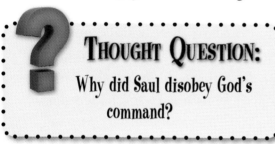

THOUGHT QUESTION:

Why did Saul disobey God's command?

Saul was rejected as the king of Israel because he had disobeyed. He thought that his own way was better than God's plan. He failed because he did not believe that to obey is better than offering sacrifices. Samuel felt very sad that Saul had lost his throne. He returned to his home in Ramah and never saw Saul again.

DAVID THE GIANT SLAYER

1 Samuel 16; 17

Samuel grieved over Saul because the king had failed to obey God. The old prophet loved him, and he had dreamed that this man would lead Israel to victory. But now there was no hope for his success. Soon the Lord spoke to Samuel: "How long will you mourn for Saul, seeing I have rejected him from reigning over Israel? Fill your horn with oil, and go; I am sending you to Jesse the Bethlehemite. For I have provided Myself a king among his sons."

The prophet thought about his own safety and said, "How can I go? If Saul hears it, he will kill me."

Then the Lord told Samuel to travel to Bethlehem with an offering. When he arrived in the town he was to say that he'd come to make a sacrifice and then invite Jesse to attend.

The prophet came to Bethlehem, and the chief men of the village saw him. Trembling with fear, they asked Samuel, "Do you come peaceably?"

"Peaceably; I have come to sacrifice to the Lord," Samuel said. So the men of the town gathered at the altar to worship God, and Jesse and his sons were present.

Now Jesse was the son of Obed and the grandson of Ruth, the gleaner who had married Boaz. Jesse was a sheep rancher, and he had eight sons who helped him tend the flocks.

After Samuel had offered the sacrifice, he wanted to see the sons of Jesse. Beginning with Eliab, the eldest, the prophet studied the young man carefully. He was pleased with Eliab's appearance, because he was strong and handsome. The man of God would have anointed him king of Israel right then, but the

GOD SAYS:
" 'Man looks at the outward appearance, but the Lord looks at the heart.' "–1 Samuel 16:7

Lord said, "Do not look at his appearance or at his physical stature, because I have refused him. For the Lord does not see as man sees; for man looks at the outward appearance, but the Lord looks at the heart."

Samuel looked carefully at son number two, Abinadab, and then sons three and four passed before him; but none of these was indicated as king. Then came sons five, six, and seven. They, too, passed by and were not accepted. Now the prophet was troubled, and he said to Jesse, "The Lord has not chosen these. . . . Are all the young men here?"

"There remains yet the youngest," Jesse replied, "and there he is, keeping the sheep." "Send and bring him," said Samuel. "For we will not sit down till he comes here."

David the shepherd boy was called in from the field and presented to Samuel. When the prophet saw the bright eyes and good-looking countenance of this teenager, he heard God say, "Arise, anoint him; for this is the one!" Samuel took the horn of oil and anointed the shepherd boy to be king, while his brothers and his father stood by and watched the strange ceremony.

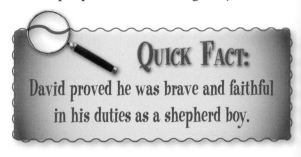

QUICK FACT:
David proved he was brave and faithful in his duties as a shepherd boy.

In the meantime, Saul had become sad and depressed. Though the king did not realize it, the Holy Spirit of God had left him for good. He began to show so many signs of mental illness that his servants made a proposal to him. A skillful harp player should be found whose soft music might soothe the king's troubled mind. Saul liked the suggestion and said, "Provide me now a man who can play well, and bring him to me."

One of the servants said, "Look, I have seen a son of Jesse the Bethlehemite, who is skillful in playing, a mighty man of valor, a man of war, prudent in speech, and a handsome person; and the Lord is with him."

Saul sent messengers to Jesse with instruction that David should come and play for him. So the father sent his boy to Saul's court with presents of fine food for the ruler. David played beautiful melodies on his harp, many of which he had composed while he herded sheep in the hills. Perhaps he sang the poem that later became the Shepherd's Psalm.

The Lord is my shepherd;
I shall not want.
He makes me to lie down in green pastures;

He leads me beside the still waters.
He restores my soul;
He leads me in the paths of righteousness
For His name's sake.

Yea, though I walk through the valley of the shadow
    of death,
I will fear no evil;
For You are with me;
Your rod and Your staff, they comfort me.

You prepare a table before me in the presence of
    my enemies;
You anoint my head with oil;
My cup runs over.
Surely goodness and mercy shall follow me
All the days of my life;
And I will dwell in the house of the Lord
Forever (Psalm 23).

Each time David played for him, Saul was refreshed by the music, and he felt happy again. He came to love David and made him his armorbearer, a high honor for a servant of the monarch.

The Philistines continued to make attacks on the people of Israel. The enemy camped on one mountain, while Israel's army was stationed on another mountain across the Valley of Elah. Every day a mighty champion from the camp of the Philistines marched down into the valley and made fun of the Israelites. His name was Goliath, and he was a giant about nine feet, nine inches tall. He wore a helmet and a coat of mail made of bronze, and he held a tall, heavy spear. His coat of mail alone weighed 57 kilograms (about 125 pounds). A soldier stayed in front of Goliath, carrying a shield. Every morning and evening for forty days, he stood before the soldiers of Israel, ridiculing them and shouting, "I defy the armies of Israel this day; give me a man, that we may fight together."

Whenever Saul and his soldiers heard the words of the Philistine, they were discouraged and afraid. Even though the king was tall and strong himself, he did not dare to fight the giant.

In the meantime, David had returned home to spend time caring for his father's sheep while three of his older brothers were in the army of Saul. One day, Jesse, who was quite old by now, said to David, "Take now for your brothers an ephah [two-thirds of a bushel] of this dried grain and these ten loaves, and run to your brothers at the camp. And carry these ten cheeses to the captain of their thousand, and see how your brothers fare, and bring back news of them."

David was anxious to go to the army of Israel and see how the fighting was going. But when he arrived at the camp he found the men in a panic because of Goliath. On hearing that no Israelite soldier was willing to challenge the giant, David volunteered. Saul heard of this and sent for the young shepherd. When questioned, David answered King Saul, "Let no man's heart fail because of him; your servant will go and fight with this Philistine."

THOUGHT QUESTION:

Why were all the Israelite soldiers afraid of Goliath?

"You are not able to go against this Philistine to fight with him," said Saul to David, "for you are a youth, and he a man of war from his youth."

"Your servant used to keep his father's sheep," David replied, "and when a lion or a bear came and took a lamb out of the flock, I went out after it and struck it, and delivered the lamb from its mouth; and when it arose against me, I caught it by its beard, and struck and killed it. Your servant has killed both lion and bear." Then David added these courageous words: "The Lord, who delivered me from the paw of the lion and from the paw of the bear, He will deliver me from the hand of this Philistine."

Saul was satisfied that David could be a valiant fighter. "Go, and the Lord be with you!" he said. He had his servants place his own heavy armor on David. Then David fastened his sword to the armor and tried to walk. He said, "I cannot walk with these, for I have not [practiced with] them." So he took off all the armor.

Picking up his shepherd's staff, and with his sling in his other hand, David marched down to the stream in the middle of the valley and carefully chose five smooth stones. He put these in his leather bag and started toward the giant. Goliath approached the young man with his shieldbearer in front of him. When he looked around and saw only young David holding a wooden staff, he shouted angrily, "Am I a dog, that you come to me with sticks?" And he cursed David by his gods.

Not at all intimidated by this snarling giant, David said to him, "You come to me with a sword, with a spear, and with a javelin. But I come to you in the name of the Lord of hosts, the God of the armies of Israel, whom you have defied. This day the Lord will deliver you into my hand, and I will strike you and take your head from you. And this day I will give the carcasses of the camp of the Philistines to the birds of the air and the wild beasts of the earth, that all the earth may know that there is a God in Israel. Then all this assembly shall know that the Lord does not save with sword and spear; for the battle is the Lord's, and He will give you into our hands."

Goliath advanced toward David, towering above the youth with his huge bulk. He pushed back his helmet in scorn, and in that moment David was ready to act. He put a stone in his sling and let it fly with all his strength and skill. The stone went straight toward Goliath's head and buried itself in his forehead! Knocked out by the blow, the giant fell forward on his face. David was not carrying a sword, so he raced over to Goliath and grabbed the giant's sword, killed him, and cut off his head.

When the Philistines saw their champion lying dead on the battlefield, they panicked and ran away in terror, leaving their tents and equipment behind. The armies of Israel rose up with a great shout and pursued the enemy and defeated them. David became the hero of his people.

DAVID FLEES FROM SAUL

1 Samuel 18–20

When David returned from his fight with Goliath the Philistine giant, Saul took him to the royal court. The king would not permit this young man to return to his home at Bethlehem, when he could be a valuable leader in the army. David was given command of a thousand soldiers. In the palace, he played sweet music on his harp when the king was sad.

When David began to live at Saul's court, he became friends with Jonathan, Saul's son. The young men grew to love each other like brothers and became best friends. Jonathan gave his cloak and his armor and sword and bow, even his belt, to David as a sign of friendship.

When the king and the shepherd returned from battle with the Philistines, the women of the city welcomed them by singing,

"Saul has slain his thousands,
And David his ten thousands."

King Saul became jealous of David when he saw how much the people loved this young hero. As David's popularity increased, the king became very angry. One day while David was playing music for Saul, the angry monarch sat with a spear in his hand. Suddenly he hurled it at the harp player, saying, "I will pin David to the wall!" But the young man escaped from the mad king, because God was with him. Feeling grieved because his father now hated David, Jonathan determined to shield his friend from danger.

Michal, Saul's younger daughter, fell in love with David, and the king consented to their marriage. Saul commanded, however, that instead of the usual dowry payment from the bridegroom's family, he wanted the young man to go and kill one hundred Philistines. By this plan Saul thought that the enemy would kill David. The Lord protected David as he went off to fulfill the pledge, however. Instead of one hundred, David killed two hundred Philistines in battle. Now the king had to keep his promise. He gave Michal to David to be his wife, and she loved him very much.

Saul had become afraid of David and was more determined than ever to destroy his son-in-law. Again the king threw his spear at David in an attempt to kill him, but once more the music player escaped and fled

GOD SAYS:
"David behaved more wisely than all the servants of Saul, so that his name became highly esteemed."
-1 Samuel 18:30

to his own house. Saul sent spies to David's home with instructions to kill him when he came out in the morning. But Michal heard of the plot and made a plan to save her husband. "If you do not save your life tonight," she warned, "tomorrow you will be killed." So, in the darkness Michal let David down from a window, and he slipped away to Samuel's house at Ramah.

Soon after this Saul sent a message to David, assuring him

that he would make peace; but David did not have faith in the king's word. David met Jonathan secretly and said to him, "What have I done? What is my iniquity, and what is my sin before your father, that he seeks my life?"

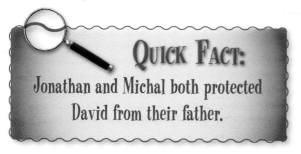

QUICK FACT:

Jonathan and Michal both protected David from their father.

Jonathan did not have an answer to that question, but he said very firmly, "By no means! You shall not die! Indeed, my father will do nothing either great or small without first telling me."

"But truly, as the Lord lives and as your soul lives," exclaimed David, "there is but a step between me and death."

Jonathan said he would do anything David asked, so David shared a plan with him. A sacred feast was to be held in the king's court the following day, and David and Jonathan were expected to sit at the king's table. David was afraid to appear, however, because of Saul's treachery. The two friends decided that Jonathan should go to the feast and David would hide in a field near the king's banquet hall. If Saul asked where David was, Jonathan would say that he had gone to Bethlehem to attend a sacrifice with his family. If the king seemed to be pleased, they could be sure it was safe for David to return to court. If the king was angry, however, they would know that the jealousy and hatred still burned in his heart.

Jonathan asked David to go with him to the field near the royal court. Jonathan said he would shoot three arrows into the field and then send a young boy after them. David would listen in his hiding place for what Jonathan called out to the boy. If the king's son said, "Look, the arrows are on this side of you; get them and come," then David was safe. If Jonathan said to the boy, "Look, the arrows are beyond you—go your way, for the Lord has sent you away," David would know that he must run for his life.

Jonathan went to the king's hall, and on the first day of the feast Saul did not ask about David. However, on the second day, when he saw the seat still empty, he asked, "Why has the son of Jesse not come to eat, either yesterday or today?"

Jonathan said to his father, "David earnestly asked permission of me to go to Bethlehem. And he said, 'Please let me go, for our family has a sacrifice in the city, and my brother has commanded me to be there. And now, if I have found favor in your eyes, please let me get away and see my brothers.' Therefore he has not come to the king's table."

When Saul heard these words, his anger flared up against Jonathan, and he picked up his spear and threw it at his own son. Jonathan dodged out of the way, however. On the third morning he went out into the field, accompanied by a small boy.

Jonathan said to the boy, "Now run, find the arrows which I shoot."

As the lad ran, Jonathan shot an arrow beyond him and shouted, "Is not the arrow beyond you? . . . Make haste, hurry, do not delay!"

THOUGHT QUESTION:
Why was Saul afraid of David?

Quickly the boy gathered up the arrows and brought them back to Jonathan. Then the man commanded the boy to carry the bow and arrows into the town. The boy went on his way not knowing that the shooting of the arrows had been a signal for David to flee from Saul. But before the shepherd of Bethlehem departed, he came out of his hiding place behind a heap of stones and said Goodbye to his friend. Afterward, Jonathan returned to the king's court, but David fled for his life—a fugitive from King Saul.

DAVID AND HIS MIGHTY MEN

1 Samuel 21–24; 2 Samuel 23:14–17

David felt lonely and forsaken after he left Jonathan. Where should he go? What should he do? He knew he was an outcast, a man hunted by the king's soldiers. Scarcely realizing where he was going, David made his way along the road that led to the city of Nob. It was in that town that the tent of meeting had been set up after the golden ark was taken by the Philistines.

Making his way to the tent of meeting, David met Ahimelech, the high priest. The man of God trembled when he saw David. He recognized that this was the brave warrior who had killed the giant Goliath. The priest remembered, too, that the giant's sword, a trophy of the great victory over the enemy, was in the tent of meeting. David asked Ahimelech for food, but he did not reveal to the high priest that he was trying to escape from King Saul.

"There is no common bread on hand," said Ahimelech, "but there is holy bread, if the young men have at least kept themselves from women." The priest gave David the sacred bread from the golden table in the Holy Place of the tent of meeting. Since the fugitive had no weapon, he asked the aged priest, "Is there not here on hand a spear or a sword?"

"The sword of Goliath the Philistine, whom you killed in the Valley of Elah, there it is, wrapped in a cloth behind the ephod," said the priest. "If you will take that, take it. For there is no other except that one here."

And David said, "There is none like it; give it to me."

Ahimelech had no idea that he was helping an enemy of King Saul. He knew David was Saul's armorbearer, so he thought he was pleasing the monarch when he gave this young warrior food and a sword and helped him on his journey.

Now, Doeg, the king's chief shepherd, happened to be in the tent of meeting, and he saw what the priest had given David. He immediately carried the news to Saul.

David pushed on toward the southwest and finally reached the Cave of Adullam. Soon his father and brothers came to the cave. They were afraid that Saul would try to kill them because of his hatred for David. The brave warrior arranged for his family to live with the king of Moab in the land where his great-grandmother Ruth was born.

Since David was an outlaw, other men began flocking to him for protection. Men in trouble for debts and other difficulties, they offered him their allegiance. Soon the Cave of Adullam was the camp for about four hundred men who were loyal to their leader.

Word that David was hiding in a cave reached Saul, and he made plans at once to surround it and kill the fugitive. But David heard of the king's plan and led his band of men to new hiding places where they could not be trapped by the royal army.

When Saul heard that Ahimelech the high priest had given food and a sword to David, he commanded that all the priests of Nob should be killed. The old priest of the Lord tried to explain to the king that he was innocent, but Saul would not listen to reason. All the priests were killed except Abiathar, a son of Ahimelech. He escaped, found David, and told him what had happened. David remembered how he had deceived the high priest by not explaining the danger he was in, and he was sorry for his terrible mistake. He said to Abiathar, "I knew that day, when Doeg the Edomite was there, that he would surely tell Saul. I have caused the death of all the persons of your father's house. Stay with me; do not

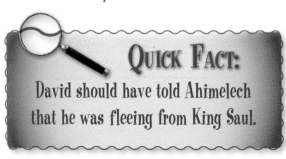

QUICK FACT:
David should have told Ahimelech that he was fleeing from King Saul.

fear. For he who seeks my life seeks your life, but with me you shall be safe."

Still hunted by King Saul, David found no safe place to hide for long. He heard that the Philistines had attacked the Israelites at Keilah, so he led his warriors against the enemy and saved the town from ruin. However, the king of Israel was in hot pursuit, so David hurried his men into the wild regions of Ziph, where they were safe for the moment. In this mountainous wilderness, Jonathan found his friend and cheered

THOUGHT QUESTION:
Why didn't David kill King Saul in the cave when he had the chance?

him with words of courage. He said, "Do not fear, for the hand of Saul my father shall not find you. You shall be king over Israel, and I shall be next to you. Even my father Saul knows that." Jonathan loved his friend so much that he was willing to give up his claim to the throne of Israel in order that David, who had been chosen by the Lord, might be the ruler.

When Saul heard that David was in the desert of En Gedi, he led his army of three thousand men in search of him. As the warriors were climbing the mountains, King Saul entered a cave to rest. Now, who should be hiding in that cave but David and his warriors. Of course, David's men quietly urged him to kill his enemy, but the young leader refused. He said he would not kill the man whom the Lord had anointed king. He did, however, steal up to Saul while he was resting and cut off a part of the king's robe.

As Saul left the cave, David called out to him, "Why do you listen to the words of men who say, 'Indeed David seeks your harm'? Look, this day your eyes have seen that the Lord delivered you today into my hand in the cave, and someone urged me to kill you. But my eye spared you."

Saul looked at his robe and saw that a piece had been cut from it. Then David said, "Let the Lord judge between you and me, and let the Lord avenge me on you. But my hand shall not be against you."

Saul looked into the darkness of the cave and said, "Is this your voice, my son David?"

Then Saul began to weep. He said to David, "You are more righteous than I; for you have rewarded me with good, whereas I have rewarded you with evil."

Then Saul and David made peace, and the king returned to his home.

David now had a band of mighty men who were daring fighters. They were completely loyal to their leader. Some of their heroic deeds are recorded in the Bible.

Once while David was far from home, his men heard him say, "Oh, that someone would give me a drink of the water from the well of Bethlehem, which is by the gate!"

Three of his men slipped away from the camp, went through the enemy lines, and got a pitcher of water from that well. When they brought the water to David, and he realized the grave danger they had faced to get it, he would not drink it. He poured it on the ground as an offering to the Lord.

God Says:

" 'You are more righteous than I; for you have rewarded me with good, whereas I have rewarded you with evil.' " -1 Samuel 24:17

SAUL'S LAST BATTLE

1 Samuel 28:3–2 Samuel 1:27

The whole nation mourned when Samuel died, because the prophet had been a strong leader in Israel. From the day his mother, Hannah, brought him to the tent of meeting when he was a small boy, he had obeyed the Lord and served Him faithfully. He had been a good and fair judge, urging the people to do right.

The menacing armies of the Philistines gathered together once more and camped on the plain of Jezreel, the place where Gideon had once won a victory with his three hundred men. King Saul felt afraid and wished he could talk to Samuel so he might know what to do to save the nation. But now the prophet was dead, and the Lord would not answer the inquiries of the rejected ruler.

Although Saul had ridden Israel of all the spirit mediums and witches in earlier years, now he was desperate and wanted to find one who might help him talk to Samuel. The king's servants reported that a woman at En Dor claimed to be able to speak to the dead. Of course, she could not bring back to life the dead people asleep in their graves, but she could communicate with evil spirits and deceive Saul.

Wearing ordinary army gear as a disguise, the king and two of his guards rode at night to the spirit medium's hiding place in a cave at En Dor. Saul said, "Please conduct a séance for me, and bring up for me the one I shall name to you."

The woman was afraid when she saw the three visitors and, not realizing who she was speaking to, exclaimed that King Saul had ordered all the mediums to be killed. But the king promised her, "As the Lord lives, no punishment shall come upon you for this thing."

The woman asked, "Whom shall I bring up for you?"

"Bring up Samuel for me," Saul requested.

When a ghostlike figure appeared that looked like Samuel, the woman screamed and said, "Why have you deceived me? For you are Saul!"

"Do not be afraid," said the king. "What did you see?"

GOD SAYS:

"Saul answered, 'I am deeply distressed; for the Philistines make war against me, and God has departed from me and does not answer me anymore.' " -1 Samuel 28:15

The woman declared that she had seen an old man coming up out of the earth. Although she did not know it, the apparition was not Samuel, but an evil spirit. It spoke a warning that defeat and death were coming to Saul. When the king heard this, he fell to the ground, weak and frightened, and his servants were afraid that he would die. The spirit medium prepared some food, and after the king had eaten and rested, he was able to get up and return to his army.

The next morning the armies of Israel and the Philistines clashed on the plain. The princes of the Philistines pushed their army forward so hard that the men of Israel could not stop them.

Finally King Saul's soldiers broke and ran away, and the Philistines overtook them on Mount Gilboa. In the raging battle, Jonathan and his two brothers were killed,

THOUGHT QUESTION:
Could the witch really talk to dead people?

and the king was severely wounded. When Saul saw that the enemy would be able to capture him, he fell on his own sword and died.

David and his warriors did not fight in this battle. They were camped at the town of Ziklag. Two days after the battle, a messenger from the king's army came to David. The man had dust on his head, and his clothes were torn. He bowed low, and David the outlaw asked, "Where have you come from?"

"I have escaped from the camp of Israel," the man replied.

"How did the matter go? Please tell me," David said.

"The people have fled from the battle, many of the people are fallen and dead, and Saul and Jonathan his son are dead also."

Then David took hold of his clothes and tore them, and all the men who were with him did the same thing. This was the customary way for the people of those days to show their sorrow. The band of warriors fasted and wept until that evening.

Memories came to David's mind of his deep friendship with Jonathan and, in better days, King Saul. Taking his harp, the man who had comforted Saul with his

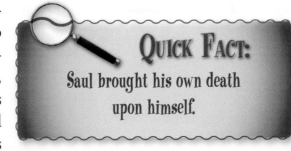

QUICK FACT:
Saul brought his own death upon himself.

music now sang a beautiful lament for the loss of the king and his son. The song ended with these mournful lines:

"O daughters of Israel, weep over Saul,
Who clothed you in scarlet, with luxury;
Who put ornaments of gold on your apparel.

How the mighty have fallen in the midst of the battle!
Jonathan was slain in your high places.
I am distressed for you, my brother Jonathan;
You have been very pleasant to me;
Your love to me was wonderful,
Surpassing the love of women.

How the mighty have fallen,
And the weapons of war perished!"

DAVID IS CROWNED KING

2 Samuel 2:1–6:19

The death of Saul made it possible for David to return safely to his own country. He knew that God had chosen him to be ruler of Israel after Saul, but he was not certain what he should do to win the hearts of the people. The Lord instructed David to go to Hebron, the chief city of Judah.

When David marched into Hebron with six hundred warriors and their families and possessions, he was welcomed by the men of the city. Since David was from the tribe of Judah, the men of that tribe were proud to have him rule over them, and they anointed him king.

David's kingship had scarcely been announced when Abner, commander of Saul's army, proclaimed that Ishbosheth, a son of Saul, was king. This rival ruler made his headquarters at Mahanaim, a town on the east side of

QUICK FACT:
David didn't force the other tribes of Israel to accept him as king.

the Jordan River. For more than two years, Israel had two kings. Then quarreling broke out among Saul's men, and Abner was killed. Soon afterward Ishbosheth was murdered by his own guards. Only then did all of the tribes of Israel come to David in Hebron and proclaim him their king.

On the coronation day, vivid memories must have come to David. He had suffered through years of hardship and danger since the time his father had called him from sheepherding to be anointed by Samuel. Now, at thirty years of age, David stood before the vast assembly of his people. Priests, soldiers, and leaders from all the tribes watched as the son of Jesse, now dressed in royal robes, knelt down and the crown was placed on his head.

It was time to choose a capital city near the center of the kingdom. After studying the situation, David selected the mountain city of Jerusalem, a stronghold of the Jebusites that the armies of Israel had never conquered. The king led his soldiers against the fortress, and they captured it. Thus, Jerusalem became the City of David, and here the king built his palace.

The Philistines, who knew David well from his outlaw days, heard that he had become king of all Israel. Thinking they could defeat the young king, they gathered an army against the new ruler in the Valley of Rephaim, only a short distance from Jerusalem. David asked the Lord what he should do in this emergency. "Shall I go up against the Philistines? Will You deliver them into my hand?" he prayed to God.

The Lord gave him a clear answer: "Go up, for I will doubtless deliver the Philistines into your hand." So the king led his soldiers against the enemy and defeated them.

But this did not discourage the Philistines, who did not know when to give up. Once more they came up against Israel in the Valley of Rephaim, and again David asked the Lord what he should do. This time he was told, "You shall not go up; circle around behind them, and come upon them in front of the mulberry trees. So it shall be, when you hear the sound of marching in the tops of the mulberry trees, then you shall advance quickly. For then the Lord will go out before you to strike the camp of the Philistines."

David did as God commanded, and the enemy was defeated and driven out of the land of Israel. Never again during the reign of David did the Philistines trouble the people of Israel.

As peace came to the country, the king was determined to bring the golden ark to Jerusalem. It had remained in the house of Abinadab since the day the Philistines sent it back to Israel on an oxcart. The king summoned thirty thousand prominent men from the twelve tribes to join him in the royal procession. They marched to Abinidab's house at Kirjath-jearim, nine miles from Jerusalem. Priests placed the ark on a new cart drawn by oxen, and the thousands of people followed, singing songs and playing musical instruments.

Two sons of Abinadab, Uzzah and Ahio, drove the cart. As the cart was moving along the rough road, the oxen stumbled, and the sacred ark shook

GOD SAYS:

"David was thirty years old when he began to reign, and he reigned forty years." –2 Samuel 5:4

and slid so much it looked as if it might fall off. No one except the priests was allowed to touch this holy object, on pain of death. But Uzzah, who was walking beside the cart, reached out and took hold of the ark to steady it. "Then the anger of the Lord was aroused against Uzzah, and God struck him there for his error; and he died there by the ark of God." If David had followed the Lord's instructions concerning the ark, he would have had the priests carry it to Jerusalem in the same way they had in the time of Moses, and this divine judgment would not have fallen on Uzzah.

? THOUGHT QUESTION:
Why did God kill Uzzah for touching the ark when he was only trying to save it from falling?

The king and the people were afraid because of the sudden death of this man, and David realized that he did not know how he should take the golden ark to his capital city. He left the ark in the house of a farmer, Obed-Edom the Gittite, and the procession of thousands returned to Jerusalem.

Three months later the king called the leaders together again. With priests to perform the sacred work of carrying the ark, the procession marched from Obed-Edom's house to Jerusalem, where David held a special service of thanksgiving. The golden ark was placed in the tent David had prepared, and the people blessed the name of the Lord. Then the king gave every man and woman a loaf of bread, a piece of meat, and a cake of raisins, and they went home rejoicing that such a good king ruled over Israel.

A KINDNESS AND A CRIME

2 Samuel 9:1–12:23

T he memory of his close friendship with Jonathan lingered in King David's mind. He wanted to do a kind deed to a member of Saul's family as a token of his enduring love. One day the king asked his advisors, "Is there still anyone who is left of the house of Saul, that I may show him kindness for Jonathan's sake?"

Royal servants soon found a man named Ziba who had been a servant in Saul's palace. When he was brought before David, he said, "There is still a son of Jonathan who is lame in his feet."

"Where is he?" the king asked.

Ziba told David that Mephibosheth, the son of Jonathan, lived at Lo Debar. The king sent for him at once; but when the crippled man came to the royal court, he was fearful. Perhaps he thought that David would kill him because he was a grandson of Saul.

> ## GOD SAYS:
> " 'Do not fear, for I will surely show you kindness for Jonathan your father's sake.' " -2 Samuel 9:7

"Do not fear," said David to him, "for I will surely show you kindness for Jonathan your father's sake, and will restore to you all the land of Saul your grandfather; and you shall eat bread at my table continually."

Such kindness was more than Mephibosheth could have ever expected. From that day on, he lived in the king's palace and ate at David's table like one of his sons.

For many years David served Israel faithfully, and he loved the Lord of heaven. After he had built his palace at Jerusalem, however, he committed a crime. He saw a beautiful woman and wanted her to be his wife. The woman, named Bathsheba, was already married to Uriah, a soldier in the king's army. David instructed the chief of the army to place Uriah at the front of a battle so that he would almost certainly be killed. After word came to the king that Uriah had died, he married Bathsheba.

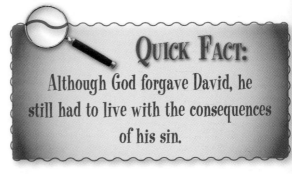

QUICK FACT:
Although God forgave David, he still had to live with the consequences of his sin.

David thought that his awful deed was a secret he could keep from everyone; but God, who sees everything we do, had made a record of it. A day came when the Lord gave Nathan, who was a prophet in Israel, a message to deliver to David. The prophet appeared before the king and told him a parable:

"There were two men in one city, one rich and the other poor. The rich man had exceedingly many flocks and herds. But the poor man had nothing, except one little ewe lamb which he had bought and nourished; and it grew up together with him and with his children. It ate of his own food and drank from his own cup and lay in his bosom; and it was like a daughter to him. And a traveler came to the rich man, who

refused to take from his own flock and from his own herd to prepare one [lamb] for the wayfaring man who had come to him; but he took the poor man's lamb and prepared it for the man who had come to him."

King David was angry when he heard the prophet's story. He said, "As the Lord lives, the man who has done this shall surely die! And he shall restore fourfold for the lamb, because he did this thing and because he had no pity."

The prophet looked at the king of Israel and said, "You are the man! Thus says the Lord God of Israel: . . . 'You have killed Uriah the Hittite with the sword; you have taken his wife to be your wife, and have killed him with the sword of the people of Ammon. Now therefore, the sword shall never depart from your house, because you have despised Me, and have taken the wife of Uriah the Hittite to be your wife.' "

When David married Bathsheba, he thought that no one would ever know he had caused Uriah to be killed. But now the prophet of God stood before the king, revealing that he was a murderer.

With a humble, sorrowful heart David said, "I have sinned against the Lord."

"The Lord also has put away your sin; you

THOUGHT QUESTION: What did the story of the poor man's lamb teach David?

shall not die," the prophet replied. God is wonderful to forgive our rebellious deeds so that they will not be held against us!

A son was born to David and Bathsheba, but he became very sick. The king fasted and cried and pleaded with God that the child might live. All night he lay on the hard ground and would not get up. Seven days after the little boy fell ill, he died. David got up, washed and dressed, and went to the house of God to worship. The sorrowing king had repented of the crime he had committed, and God forgave him. He returned to the palace, and his servants of the royal household set food in front of him, and he ate.

ABSALOM, A REBELLIOUS SON

2 Samuel 15:1–19:8

Trouble arose in David's family, just as the prophet Nathan had predicted. As the king's oldest sons grew to manhood, conflicts flared up between the ruler and his sons, and among the sons themselves. David had failed to teach his children to obey when they were young; and when they did wrong, he was afraid to punish them.

Absalom, one of David's sons, had grown up into a handsome prince. He was proud of his thick, beautiful hair. In fact, it was so heavy that he trimmed off more than three pounds of hair when he cut it each year.

The young prince was selfish and headstrong. He quarreled with his brothers and dreamed of the day when he might be king. He became impatient, however, and as his ambition grew, he decided that he would seize the kingship from his father.

Proud Absalom rode around Jerusalem in a chariot drawn by fine horses, while fifty men ran in front of him to clear the streets. Soon the prince became a celebrity, able to draw the attention of many people. He was clever and crafty too. He would get up early in the morning and go to the city gate, where men of Israel entered who wanted to see the king about a complaint or a lawsuit. Absalom would stop the travelers, ask about their home and family, and listen to their stories. He pretended to sympathize with them in their trouble. Then he would say slyly, "Oh, that I were made judge in the land, and everyone who has any suit or cause would come to me; then I would give him justice." Whenever a man bowed before him, the prince would put out his hand and take hold of him and kiss him. In this way Absalom won the hearts of many people in Israel.

> ### GOD SAYS:
> "So Absalom stole the hearts of the men of Israel." –2 Samuel 15:6

Now David did not know that his son was trying to take the throne from him. But after four years of drawing the people to follow him, Absalom decided to act. The prince went to his father and deceived him by saying, "Please, let me go to Hebron and pay the vow which I made to the Lord."

"Go in peace," the king said.

When Absalom arrived in Hebron, he sent secret messengers to the leaders of the twelve tribes, calling on them to revolt against King David. Gradually the prince gathered an army that was loyal to him. The next thing David knew, a messenger came to the palace saying that the rebellious son had made himself king of Israel.

When David heard this, he was frightened and said, "Arise, and let us flee, or we shall not escape from Absalom. Make haste to depart, lest he overtake us suddenly and bring disaster upon us, and strike the city with the edge of the sword."

The king left his palace hurriedly with his entire household and a band of his faithful warriors. The people of Jerusalem flooded out of the city to avoid being caught in a battle. People in the countryside wept as they saw the king's entourage pass by. Led by Abiathar and Zadok, the priests carried the precious golden ark along the road.

When the king and his people stopped to rest, he said to Zadok the priest, "Carry the ark of God back into the city. If I find favor in the eyes of the Lord, He will bring me back and show me both it and His dwelling place. . . . I will wait in the plains of the wilderness until word comes from you to inform me."

As he climbed the road leading over the Mount of Olives, King David wept. His head was covered as a sign of mourning, and he walked barefoot. Through the night the king's company fled eastward, making their way down the rocky, desolate slopes to the Jordan River. Ziba, Mephibosheth's servant, brought food for the fugitives and mules for the king and his family members to ride on.

Hushai, a trusted counselor of King David, had joined the royal party as it left the city. The king now sent his friend back to the palace, and when Absalom captured Jerusalem without a struggle, Hushai pretended to offer his service. This pleased the prince, and he listened to Hushai's advice. Absalom had planned to send an army at once in pursuit of his father, but Hushai was determined to delay this action so that the king would have time to gather his warriors and fight.

THOUGHT QUESTION: Why did King David send the ark back to Jerusalem?

"You know your father and his men," Hushai said to Absalom, "that they are mighty men, and they are enraged in their minds, like a bear robbed of her cubs in the field; and your father is a man of war, and will not camp with the people. Surely by now he is hidden in some pit, or in some other place. And it will be, when some of them are overthrown at the first, that whoever hears it will say, 'There is a slaughter among the people who follow Absalom.' And even he who is valiant, whose heart is like the heart of a lion, will melt completely. For all Israel knows that your father is a mighty man, and those who are with him are valiant men.

"Therefore I advise that all Israel be fully gathered to you, from Dan to Beersheba, like the sand that is by the sea for multitude, and that you go to battle in person. So we will come upon him in some place where he may be found, and we will fall on him as the dew falls on the ground. And of him and all the men who are with him there shall not be left so much as one."

QUICK FACT:
Just as David loved his son Absalom, God loves us even when we rebel against him.

Absalom liked this counsel and accepted it. Then Hushai sent a secret message to David telling him to cross the Jordan River with his followers and find safety in a walled city.

That night, everyone who had accompanied David crossed the river. The king made plans with Joab, his general, to divide the small loyal army into three groups in order to fight Absalom's forces. The king loved his son in spite of his rebellion, and when the battle was about to be fought, David gave instructions to his three chief officers, Joab, Abishai, and Ittai, saying, "Deal gently for my sake with the young man Absalom."

The fight took place in the forest of Ephraim. David's warriors routed the army of Absalom and won a great victory. Prince Absalom was riding through the forest on a mule when he happened to meet some of David's men. The prince rode under a giant oak tree, and his head got caught in the thick branches. While David's men watched, the mule galloped off, leaving Absalom hanging in midair. When a servant told Joab of Absalom's plight, the general hurried to the oak tree and killed the rebel prince with three spears.

As the trumpets sounded victory for King David, the soldiers stopped fighting on the battlefield. When they came to General Joab, they saw the body of Absalom in the tree. After taking it down, they cast the body into a deep pit. Then they piled a great heap of stones over the grave of the traitor.

Joab knew that the news of the victory must be sent to King David, who was sitting at the gate in the nearby town of Mahanaim. Ahimaaz, the son of Zadok the priest, wanted to run with the message, but Joab told a Cushite follower who had seen all that had happened to go and tell the king about the battle. Ahimaaz was unhappy that he wasn't chosen, so Joab gave him permission to run to the king behind the Cushite.

Ahimaaz was a swift runner, and he passed the Cushite; but when he came to the king he had no message. He bowed before King David and said, "All is well."

"Is the young man Absalom safe?" asked the king anxiously.

"I saw great confusion just as Joab was about to send the king's servant and me, your servant, but I don't know what it was," explained Ahimaaz.

"Stand aside and wait here," said the king. At that moment the Cushite entered. He said, "My Lord the king, hear the good news! The Lord has delivered you today from all who rose up against you."

Then the king asked the messenger, "Is the young man Absalom safe?"

The Cushite broke the news gently by saying, "May the enemies of my Lord the king and all who rise up to harm you be like that young man."

The king was shaken and went to the room above the gateway

to weep. As he climbed the steps he cried, "O my son Absalom—my son, my son Absalom—if only I had died in your place! O Absalom my son, my son!"

Soon the monarch returned to his palace at Jerusalem and continued to reign over the tribes of Israel.

SOLOMON BUILDS THE TEMPLE

1 Kings 1:15–12:24

When King David had grown old and feeble, he chose his son Solomon to be king in his place. Now Adonijah, another of David's sons, was determined that he would be the ruler on the throne. He planned a feast and invited all his brothers except Solomon to attend. Nathan the prophet and Zadok the priest heard of this plot. They hurried to the palace and told Bathsheba, David's wife. The king was lying in bed, sick, and rarely got up anymore. When his wife came to him and told him of the evil plot to usurp the throne, the aged warrior called Nathan and Zadok to him and commanded them to anoint Solomon as king of Israel.

The two leaders took Solomon to the town of Gihon. Zadok the priest anointed Solomon, the trumpets sounded, and the people who were gathered around shouted, "Long live King Solomon!" Soon the people of Jerusalem heard that Solomon had been proclaimed king, and when he arrived there, they showed their allegiance to him, playing flutes and singing and celebrating so loudly that it shook the ground.

The guests at Adonijah's feast heard the sounds of celebration and asked, "Why is the city in such a noisy uproar?"

At that moment Jonathan the son of Abiathar arrived and Adonijah said to him, "Come in, for you are a prominent man, and bring good news."

GOD SAYS:
" 'As the Lord has been with my Lord the king, even so may He be with Solomon.' " -1 Kings 1:37

"No!" the messenger replied. "Our Lord King David has made Solomon king. The king has sent with him Zadok the priest, Nathan the prophet, Benaiah the son of Jehoiada, the Cherethites, and the Pelethites; and they have made him ride on the king's mule. So Zadok the priest and Nathan the prophet have anointed him king at Gihon; and they have gone up from there rejoicing, so that the city is in an uproar. This is the noise that you have heard."

When the sons of David and the other guests heard this alarming news, they left the feast in a hurry. Afraid for his life now, Adonijah rushed to the tent of meeting and took hold of the horns of the altar. Solomon sent men to bring Adonijah to him; the brother bowed before the king and promised complete loyalty to him.

Before David died, he called the new king to him and gave him a challenge. "I go the way of all the earth," David said to Solomon. "Be strong, therefore, and prove yourself a man. And keep the charge of the Lord your God: to walk in His ways, to keep His statutes, His commandments, His judgments, and His testimonies, as it is written in the Law of Moses, that you may prosper in all that you do and wherever you turn; that the Lord may fulfill His word which He spoke concerning me, saying, 'If your sons take heed to their way, to walk before Me in truth with all their heart and with all their soul,' He said, 'you shall not lack a man on the throne of Israel.' "

David had dreamed of building a beautiful temple in which the Lord could live with His people. But the king had been a man of war, and there was a lot of fighting and rebellion during his reign. God told him that the temple construction must be left to Solomon. To make his son's task easier, the faithful old king had plans made for the house of God. He also gathered building materials: silver, gold, brass, and precious stones. King David died after ruling Israel for forty years, and he was buried in Jerusalem.

Solomon loved the Lord God and followed the good counsel of his father. One night God appeared to him in a dream and said, "Ask! What shall I give you?"

What would *you* choose if you could have anything in the world? Would you be as careful in your choice as this young king was?

Solomon asked for wisdom and understanding. He wanted to judge his people with justice and have the ability to see the difference between good and evil. The Lord was so pleased with the king's request that He not only gave Solomon wisdom, but He also blessed him with great riches and power. The king wrote three thousand proverbs and composed more than a thousand songs. He knew many things about trees, flowers, animals, birds, fish, and reptiles. Men came to him from other nations to learn from his great wisdom.

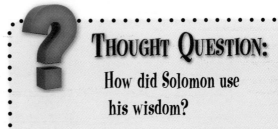

THOUGHT QUESTION:
How did Solomon use his wisdom?

The Queen of Sheba came to visit the king of Israel. She

saw his palace and his great wealth. She also heard his wise sayings, and she said to Solomon, "It was a true report which I heard in my own land about your words and your wisdom. However I did not believe the words until I came and saw with my own eyes; and indeed the half was not told me. Your wisdom and prosperity exceed the fame of which I heard."

The queen gave Solomon gold, spices, and precious stones. In return Solomon presented many gifts to the Queen of Sheba. The record says that he gave her "all she desired, whatever she asked." Then she returned to her own land with her courtiers and servants.

The time had come to build the temple. Hiram, king of Tyre, was a friend of David, and he supplied Solomon with

cedar and other choice lumber needed for the building. Thousands of men were sent into the mountains of Lebanon to cut down trees. Other thousands cut and squared great stones and polished them for the building. King Hiram also sent to Solomon skilled craftsmen who could carve wood and engrave in silver, gold, and brass. Weavers spent months and years making rich, beautiful tapestries. While the house of God was being erected, no sound of a hammer, an ax, or any iron tool was heard within it. All the stones were prepared at the quarry, and the wood and metal were made ready before they were brought to the temple site.

After seven years of constant labor, Solomon's workers finished the beautiful house of God. The golden ark and the other furniture were brought from the tent of meeting to the temple. The king set a time for the dedication service, and he invited the people from all over the nation to witness the event. First the priests offered lavish sacrifices. Then they blew their trumpets, and finally they entered the Holy Place. The cloud of glory of the Lord filled the temple with such splendor that the priests could not perform their service.

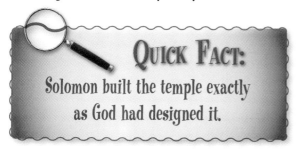

Quick Fact:
Solomon built the temple exactly as God had designed it.

Then the king blessed all the people. As he stood before the altar, he raised his arms toward heaven and said, "Lord God of Israel, there is no God in heaven above or on earth below like You, who keep Your covenant and mercy with Your servants who walk before You with all their hearts. You have kept what You promised Your servant David my father; You have both spoken with Your mouth and fulfilled it with Your hand, as it is this day."

The king also asked God to bless and guide the nation in times of war or famine caused by rebellion in Israel, and to forgive and forget the people's sins.

For seven days the nation celebrated the dedication of the temple with sacrifices and feasting. On the eighth day Solomon sent the people back to their homes, and everyone rejoiced because of the goodness of the Lord God.

Solomon spent thirteen years building a magnificent palace for himself, and also a beautiful home for one of his wives, the daughter of Pharaoh in Egypt. The king of Israel had stables for forty thousand horses. He had fleets of ships in the Red Sea and in the Mediterranean Sea. The royal navy sailed to far countries and returned with gold, silver, ivory, apes, and peacocks. The record states that the king made silver in Jerusalem as common as stone and cedar trees as plentiful as the sycamore trees that grew on the foothills.

In spite of riches and fame, the reign of Solomon did not end in glory. Luxury and wealth were too much even for this wise man. He married many wives from foreign nations, and their heathen religions turned the king's heart from serving the Lord. Enemies rose up against Israel, and the twelve tribes quarreled among themselves. The Lord reproved Solomon in these words: "Because you have done this, and have not kept My covenant and My statutes, which I have commanded you, I will surely tear the kingdom away from you and give it to your servant. Nevertheless I will not do it in your days, for the sake of your father David; I will tear it out of the hand of your son. However I will not tear away the whole kingdom; I will give one tribe to your son for the sake of My servant David, and for the sake of Jerusalem which I have chosen."

By this message Solomon knew that the nation would never be strong and united again. The king reigned over Israel for forty years; and when he died, he was buried in Jerusalem. Rehoboam, the son of Solomon, took the throne of his father.

During Solomon's reign the people had been forced to pay heavy taxes. When Rehoboam became king, the leaders begged him to lighten their burdens. However, the young king refused to listen to the counsel of the older

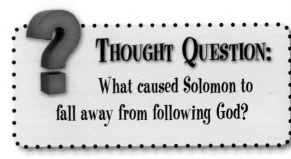

THOUGHT QUESTION:
What caused Solomon to fall away from following God?

men. He said to the people, "My father made your yoke heavy, but I will add to your yoke; my father chastised you with whips, but I will chastise you with [scorpions]!"

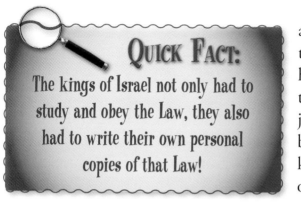

QUICK FACT:
The kings of Israel not only had to study and obey the Law, they also had to write their own personal copies of that Law!

Rebellion broke out among the tribes. When the civil war ended, Rehoboam had only the tribes of Judah and Benjamin with him. This became the kingdom known as Judah. The other ten tribes chose Jeroboam for their leader, and the second kingdom was known as Israel.

From this time on, the nation was divided. The ten tribes of Israel continued for about two hundred fifty years before they were overthrown by enemies. The little nation of Judah stood for almost four hundred years, but finally it fell before the attacks of the king of Babylon. Most of the kings of Israel and Judah did evil things and ignored God. Only a few of the kings loved the Lord and led the people in the right way. Never again did the nation attain such glory and power as it had during the reign of King Solomon.

ELIJAH, FIGHTER FOR GOD

1 Kings 17:1–2 Kings 2:15

During the reign of Ahab, seventh king of Israel, a faithful representative for God suddenly appeared in the royal court. The representative was Elijah the prophet, and he came from his home in the mountains of Gilead, east of the river Jordan. He entered the court and stood before Ahab, a weak-willed and evil king. The Bible says that Ahab did more sinful things to provoke the anger of the Lord God than all the Israelite kings before him. The monarch was dominated by his heathen wife, Jezebel. She was an ambitious woman who wanted to make all of Israel wor-ship the pagan god Baal. Ahab had built a temple to Baal and placed a large wooden statue of Baal inside it.

When God saw His people sinking into idolatry, He sent Elijah to reprove the king for his terrible actions. The man of God stood before Ahab and said, "As the Lord God of Israel lives, before whom I stand, there shall not be dew nor rain these years, except at my word." Then, without waiting for a response, the prophet walked out of the court.

The king was stunned by the strange message, and he decided to kill the prophet. But the Lord was with Elijah and gave him these instructions: "Get away from here and turn eastward, and hide by the Brook Cherith, which flows into the Jordan. And it will be that you shall drink from the brook, and I have commanded the ravens to feed you there." Although Ahab sent search parties out to catch the prophet, they could not find him.

QUICK FACT:

God's message to Ahab gave Jezebel and all the followers of Baal a chance to test the power of their god.

Elijah lived in hiding beside the Cherith, a stream that flowed into the Jordan River. Every morning and evening, some ravens flew to him bringing bread and meat. As long as there was water in the stream, Elijah could stay in this safe retreat.

But a day came when the severe drought reduced the stream to a trickle of water, and then it dried up completely. God told Elijah to go to Zarephath, a northern town in the area of Sidon, outside of the kingdom of Israel. As the prophet came to the city gate, he saw a widow gathering sticks to make a fire. "Please bring me a little water in a cup, that I may drink," he called out to the woman.

As she went to get a jar of water, he called to her again, say-ing, "Please bring me a morsel of bread in your hand."

"As the Lord your God lives," she replied, "I do not have bread, only a handful of flour in a bin, and a little oil in a jar; and see, I am gathering a couple of sticks that I may go in and prepare it for myself and my son, that we may eat it, and die."

"Do not fear," said the prophet. "Go and do as you have said, but make me a small cake from it first, and bring it to me; and afterward make some for yourself and your son. For thus says the Lord God of Israel: 'The bin of flour shall not be used up, nor shall the jar of oil run dry, until the day the Lord sends rain on the earth.' "

The woman decided to trust Elijah's words, and from then on, day after day, she and her son had food to eat. There was always flour in the bin in the morning, and there was enough oil to mix with it to make cakes for her family.

The woman's young son became very sick and died. The mother came to Elijah in her grief, and the prophet said, "Give me your son."

He carried the dead child upstairs to his room and laid him on the bed. Then the prophet prayed, "O Lord my God, have You also brought tragedy on the widow with whom I lodge, by killing her son?" He stretched himself over the body three times and called on God, saying, "O Lord my God, I pray, let this child's soul come back to him." Elijah's prayer was an-swered, and the child got up immediately. The man of God took him downstairs to his mother. The happy woman said, "Now by this I know that you are a man of God, and that the word of the Lord in your mouth is the truth."

In the third year of the drought and famine, Elijah received instruction from heaven to tell King Ahab that the Lord would bring rain to the parched earth.

When the unrepentant king saw Elijah, he exclaimed angrily, "Is that you, O troubler of Israel?"

"I have not troubled Israel," the prophet said, "but you and your father's house have, in that you have forsaken the commandments of the Lord and have followed the Baals. Now therefore, send and gather all Israel to me on Mount Carmel, the four hundred and fifty prophets of Baal, and the four

hundred prophets of Asherah, who eat at Jezebel's table."

Without questioning the prophet's instruction, King Ahab sent messengers throughout the country, calling the people and the prophets of Baal to assemble on Mount Carmel. On the day Elijah came to the people on the mountain, he challenged them by saying, "How long will you falter between two opinions? If the Lord is God, follow Him; but if Baal, follow him."

The people were silent. Then Elijah said, "I alone am left a prophet of the Lord; but Baal's prophets are four hundred and fifty men. Therefore let them give us two bulls; and let them choose one bull for themselves, cut it in pieces, and lay it on the wood, but put no fire under it; and I will prepare the other bull, and lay it on the wood, but put no fire under it. Then you call on the name of your gods, and I will call on the name of the Lord; and the God who answers by fire, He is God."

The people answered him, "It is well spoken." They thought Elijah's proposal was fair.

The prophet of God told the priests of Baal that they should be first to build an altar and put their sacrifice on it. It was morning, and the priests called out to Baal continuously until noon, but nothing happened. Elijah was watching, and he mocked them a little bit, saying, "Cry aloud, for

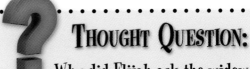

THOUGHT QUESTION:
Why did Elijah ask the widow to make a cake for him first?

he is a god; either he is meditating, or he is busy, or he is on a journey, or perhaps he is sleeping and must be awakened."

Baal's priests became more and more frantic. They shouted louder and danced around, and they slashed themselves with knives until blood gushed out of their wounds. But there was no answer from their god. They shouted and pleaded all afternoon.

In the late afternoon Elijah said to the people, "Come near to me." They crowded as close as they could. The prophet gathered twelve large stones and rebuilt the altar of the Lord that had been broken down and long forgotten. He also dug a ditch around the

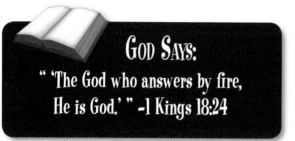

GOD SAYS:

" 'The God who answers by fire, He is God.' " –1 Kings 18:24

altar. After placing wood on the altar and then the cut-up bull for the sacrifice on top of that, the prophet directed that four jars of water be poured over the sacrifice.

The water soaked the bull and the wood and the stones. Then Elijah called for four more jars of water, and then four more. The water ran down and filled the trench around the altar.

It was now the time of day when the evening sacrifice was supposed to be offered to God. Elijah prayed, "Lord God of Abraham, Isaac, and Israel, let it be known this day that You are God in Israel and I am Your servant, and that I have done all these things at Your word. Hear me, O Lord, hear me, that this people may know that You are the Lord God, and that You have turned their hearts back to You again."

Suddenly, *Boom!* Fire flashed down from the Lord and burned the sacrifice and the wood. It consumed the stones and the dirt and licked up the water in the trench. When the people saw this awesome power from God, they fell on their faces and said, "The Lord, He is God! The Lord, He is God!"

Elijah shouted, "Seize the prophets of Baal! Do not let one of them escape!" Those evil men were executed because they had deceived the whole nation and led the people to do wicked things.

King Ahab had witnessed the power of God with his own eyes. Elijah said to him, "Go up, eat and drink; for there is the sound of abundance of rain." While the king was eating and drinking, the prophet took his servant, and together they climbed to the top of the mountain. Elijah sat down and put his face between his knees. He told the servant to go and look toward the ocean.

The servant went to scan the cloudless horizon over the blue Mediterranean Sea and then came back. "There is nothing," he said. Elijah sent the man back to look again and again, but it was not until the seventh time that he came running to Elijah and said excitedly, "There is a cloud, as small as a man's hand, rising out of the sea!"

Immediately the prophet commanded, "Go up, say to Ahab, 'Prepare your chariot, and go down before the rain stops you.' "

Soon the sky was almost black with clouds, a strong wind struck the mountainside, and then came a heavy downpour of rain! Ahab rode away from the mountain in his chariot toward Jezreel. God's Spirit came into Elijah, and, tucking the lower part of his robe up into his undergarments, the prophet began to run. He passed the king's chariot and ran in front of it all the way to the entrance of Jezreel, where Ahab had a palace. This was a distance of about twenty-eight miles.

When King Ahab reached the palace, he told Queen Jezebel that Elijah had executed all her priests of Baal. She sent a servant with a threatening message to the prophet, who lay sleeping by the city gate. "So let the gods do to me, and more also, if I do not make your life as the life of one of [the priests of Baal] by tomorrow about this time."

Fear overcame Elijah at this threat. He got up, woke his servant, and ran for his life toward the town of Beersheba. Leaving his servant at the town, he went a day's journey into the wilderness. Tired, hungry, and exhausted, the prophet finally stopped and sat down under a broom tree. He was so discouraged, he wanted to die.

Elijah fell asleep under the tree, and while he was lying there, an angel touched him and woke him up. The angel said, "Arise and eat." Turning his head, the prophet saw bread and a jar of water. He ate and drank and then went back to sleep. The angel woke him up later and gave him more food and water, saying that he would need strength for his next journey.

Elijah got up and walked southward in the wilderness, arriving after many days at Mount Horeb, where Moses had once lived. The prophet, still discouraged, found a cave in the mountainside, crawled into it, and spent the night there.

The next day a voice suddenly spoke to the prophet. "What are you doing here, Elijah?" asked the Lord.

Elijah tried to excuse his fear by saying that he was the only one left in Israel still faithful to God, and now they were trying to kill him.

The Lord told the prophet to return to his task in Israel. He informed Elijah that seven thousand loyal followers of God in Israel had not bowed to Baal. God also told him, "Elisha the son of Shaphat of Abel Meholah you shall anoint as prophet in your place."

THOUGHT QUESTION:
Why did Elijah become afraid and run away when Jezebel threatened him?

On his way back north, Elijah met the young farmer Elisha, plowing in a field. The prophet threw his cloak over the farm boy—a sign that he was called to God's service. Elisha accepted the challenge and went with the prophet to be his servant. For several years Elisha served his master. The two men visited the schools of the prophets, where young men were trained to love and serve God.

One day Elisha traveled with Elijah from Gilgal to Bethel. When they stopped at Bethel, Elijah said, "Elisha, stay here, please, for the Lord has sent me on to Jericho."

"As the Lord lives, and as your soul lives, I will not leave you!" the young man replied.

So the two went on to Jericho, where young men from the school of the prophets met them. When Elisha was alone, the students said to him, "Do you know that the Lord will take away your master from over you today?"

"Yes, I know; keep silent!" he replied.

Elijah came to his servant and said he was going on to the Jordan River, and he told Elisha that he could remain at Jericho. But the young man refused to part from his master, and the two went on together to the Jordan River. Fifty of the young men from the school followed at a distance to see what might happen. They saw Elijah strike the river with his cloak and the water divide; the two men walked across on dry ground.

As soon as they reached the other side of the river, Elijah said to Elisha, "Ask! What may I do for you, before I am taken away from you?"

"Please let a double portion of your spirit be upon me," Elisha begged.

"You have asked a hard thing," Elijah answered. "Nevertheless, if you see me when I am taken from you, it shall be so for you; but if not, it shall not be so."

As they were talking, a chariot of fire drawn by horses of fire suddenly appeared between the two men, and Elijah was caught up to heaven by a whirlwind.

As Elisha looked up, he cried out, "My father, my father, the chariot of Israel and its horsemen!" His master was gone, and in sorrow he tore his clothes in two pieces. Then he turned and

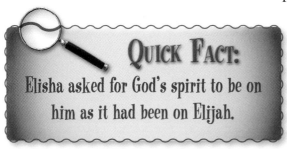

QUICK FACT:
Elisha asked for God's spirit to be on him as it had been on Elijah.

saw Elijah's cloak lying on the ground. The young man picked it up and hurried back to the Jordan River. When Elisha struck the water with the cloak, the river parted in two as it had for the mighty prophet Elijah. Then Elisha knew that he would take the place of Elijah and that God had given him power to do great work for the nation.

ELISHA, PERFORMER OF WONDERS

2 Kings 2:15–4:44; 6:1–7

Whence the sons of the prophets saw that the Lord was with Elisha, they said among themselves, "The spirit of Elijah rests on Elisha."

Elisha was a man of good deeds. He was always helping people. Before he left Jericho, the men of the city asked his advice on a practical matter. How could the spring of water that supplied the people be made fit to drink? Elisha simply took salt water and poured it into the spring, and the waters became pure and sweet.

The prophet hiked northward on the road to Bethel. While he was passing a town, a crowd of youths came out and mocked him. "Go up, you baldhead! Go up, you baldhead!" they yelled.

The prophet pronounced a curse on them in the name of the Lord, and suddenly two female bears came out of the nearby woods and mauled forty-two of them. By dishonoring the prophet Elisha, these youths were sinning against God.

One day when Elisha was home at the school of the prophets, the widow of a son of the prophets who had died came to

Elisha. "Your servant my husband is dead," she said, "and you know that your servant feared the Lord. And the creditor is coming to take my two sons to be his slaves."

"What shall I do for you?" Elisha asked. "Tell me, what do you have in the house?"

"Your maidservant has nothing in the house but a jar of oil," she answered.

"Go," he said, "borrow vessels from everywhere, from all your neighbors—empty vessels; do not gather just a few. And when you have come in, you shall shut the door behind you and your sons; then pour it into all those vessels, and set aside the full ones."

The woman followed Elisha's instructions and borrowed many empty pots. After closing her front door, she began to pour oil from her jar into the vessels, while her sons kept bringing more pots and jars to her. When all the vessels around her were full, she said to one of her sons, "Bring me another vessel."

"There is not another vessel," he replied. The widow looked in her small jar and saw that it was empty now. She hurried back to Elisha and told him that she had filled a large number of vessels with oil.

"Go, sell the oil and pay your debt," he said, "and you and your sons live on the rest."

Some time later the good prophet was walking through Shunem, a village in the hills north of Mount Carmel. As Elisha walked down the street, a prominent woman of the town saw him and invited him to her home for some food. The prophet passed through Shunem quite often, and although he didn't speak the same language as the woman and her husband, he always stopped at their home for a meal.

One day the woman said to her husband, "Look now, I know that this is a holy man of God, who passes by us regularly. Please, let us make a small upper room on the wall; and let us put a bed for him there, and a table and a chair and a lampstand; so it will be, whenever he comes to us, he can turn in there." Elisha appreciated the family's kindness in giving him a guest room, and he used it whenever he was in Shunem.

Elisha noticed that the woman had no children, and her husband was quite old. Through his servant, Gehazi, who translated for him, Elisha told the woman that God would bless her home with a son. She did not believe the prediction, but a year later, at the time Elisha had said, a baby boy was born.

THOUGHT QUESTION:
Why did God allow the bears to attack the young people who insulted Elisha?

Several years passed, and the boy grew up. One day he went out into the field where the reapers were harvesting grain. The sun's rays were hot, and the boy's head began to hurt. After a while he went to his father and cried, "My head, my head!"

The father realized that his son had sunstroke. He called a servant and said, "Carry him to his mother." The woman held the boy on her lap until noon, and then he died.

The grief-stricken mother saddled a donkey and hurried to Mount Carmel to find Elisha. She told the prophet what had happened to her only son. Elisha sent his servant Gehazi ahead of him to restore the child's life. When he came to the house, Gehazi placed Elisha's staff on the dead boy's face, as his master had instructed; but there was no sound or response from the child. He returned to Elisha with the bad news.

A short time later, Elisha arrived at the house with the woman from Shunem. He went to the upstairs room where the dead child was lying. Closing the door, he prayed to God. Then he lay down over the boy, placed his face against the child's face, and put his hands on the boy's hands. The child's skin grew warm, but he did not move. Elisha paced back and forth and prayed again. He stretched himself out on the boy once more, and suddenly the boy sneezed seven times and opened his eyes.

Elisha's servant led the mother up to the room, and when she saw her son alive and well, she bowed at the prophet's feet. "Take up your son," Elisha said. She picked up her son and went out.

Elisha went to visit another school of the prophets at Gilgal. A bad year of crops had brought famine, and

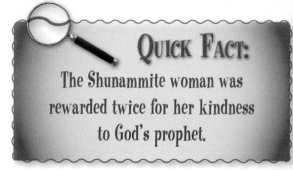

QUICK FACT:
The Shunammite woman was rewarded twice for her kindness to God's prophet.

food was scarce. Gehazi began to prepare a pot of stew for the students, and one of the young men went to the field to pick herbs. The student found some wild gourds he had never seen before. He brought them back with the herbs and sliced them into the stew pot. When the men sat down to eat, they noticed a strange taste in the food. "O man of God, there is death in the pot," they said, and they couldn't eat it.

Elisha said, "Then bring some flour," and after throwing a handful into the stew he said, "Serve it to the people, that they may eat." The pot of stew had no more poison or sour taste in it.

One day a man brought his tithe to Elisha in a knapsack. It was twenty loaves of barley bread and some fresh grain. The prophet thought at once of his hungry students. He told his servant to give it to the people of the school.

The servant asked, "What? Shall I set this before one hundred men?"

Although it seemed that twenty loaves of bread would not go far among so many men, Elisha said, "Give it to the people, that they may eat; for thus says the Lord: 'They shall eat and have some left over.' " God blessed the food, all of the people had plenty to eat, and there was some left over. Elisha always believed that God would care for His people if they trusted in Him.

GOD SAYS:

"And he showed him the place. So [Elisha] cut off a stick, and threw it in there; and he made the iron float."
-2 Kings 6:6

The sons of the prophets told Elisha that the school did not have enough room for all the students. They decided to go to the bank of the Jordan River and cut down trees for another schoolhouse. Elisha went along with the men. While they were chopping down the trees, the iron head of one student's ax flew off and fell into the river.

"Alas, master! For it was borrowed," the young man said.

"Where did it fall?" asked the man of God.

The student showed Elisha the place where the ax head had fallen into the water. The prophet cut off a stick and threw it in the water. The iron ax head floated to the surface.

"Pick it up for yourself," Elisha said. The young man reached out and took the ax head from the surface of the water.

Elisha relied on God for help in every situation, large or small, and he was never disappointed. Trust in God, and He will help you in the same way. There's no doubt about it!

A BRAVE GIRL
SAVES A LEPER

2 Kings 5

Aram, the country directly north of Israel, had made war against Israel since the days of King Ahab. During the time of Elisha the prophet, the Arameans raided the country and captured some people who lived near the city of Samaria. Among the prisoners taken to the capital city of Damascus was a girl who had seen the prophet and heard about the wonderful deeds he had done in the name of the true God.

The girl became a maid to the wife of Naaman, commander of the Aramean army. Naaman was a great man and highly respected by the king, because he had led the Aramean army to victory over the Israelites. But he was not happy, because he had the disease called leprosy. In those days there was no cure for leprosy. After some years the leper would develop a skin rash and likely lose fingers and toes because of injury or infection, and their nose might collapse. They would go blind and eventually die.

The captive Israelite maid loved Naaman's wife, and she was sad because her master had this incurable disease. One

82

day she said to her mistress, "If only my master were with the prophet who is in Samaria! For he would heal him of his leprosy."

When Naaman heard these words, he felt some hope. He decided to ask his master, the king of Aram, for permission to go to Israel in search of a cure.

"Go now," the king said, "and I will send a letter to the king of Israel." Naaman set out with chariots, horsemen, and soldiers, and he also carried ten talents of silver, six thousand shekels of gold, and ten beautiful robes as gifts for anyone who could rid him of the dread disease.

Naaman thought that the king of Israel would be able to help him. He arrived in Samaria and presented the letter from the Aramean king to the ruler of Israel. The letter read as follows: "Now be advised, when this letter comes to you, that I have sent Naaman my servant to you, that you may heal him of his leprosy."

After the Israelite king read the letter, he threw it on the floor,

QUICK FACT:
Far from her home, the little slave girl was a great witness for God.

tore his robes, and shouted, "Am I God, to kill and make alive, that this man sends a man to me to heal him of his leprosy? Therefore please consider, and see how he seeks a quarrel with me."

Elisha heard how the king of Israel had given the Syrian commander no hope of healing, and he sent a message to the king. "Why have you torn your clothes? Please let him come to me, and he shall know that there is a prophet in Israel."

So Naaman and his men rode in their chariots to the house of Elisha. The prophet did not come out to see the officer from a foreign land. Instead, he sent Gehazi, his servant, who told him, "Go and wash in the Jordan seven times, and your flesh shall be restored to you, and you shall be clean."

The Syrian commander became furious. He said, "Indeed, I said to myself, 'He will surely come out to me, and stand and call on the name of the Lord his God, and wave his hand over the place, and heal the leprosy.' Are not the

Abanah and the Pharpar, the rivers of Damascus, better than all the waters of Israel? Could I not wash in them and be clean?"

Naaman rode away from Elisha's house in a rage. When he had calmed down, one of his servants said to him, "My father, if the prophet had told you to do something great, would you not have done it? How much more then, when he says to you, 'Wash, and be clean'?"

The commander paused to think about these words. He was going to die of leprosy unless he could be healed. Why should he not follow the prophet's simple instructions?

Driving eastward until he came to the Jordan River, Naaman got down from his chariot, took off his robe, and plunged into the water. He dipped himself seven times, as Elisha had commanded. When he went down into the water, there were ugly white patches of skin and raw sores on his body. But when he rose up from the water the seventh time, Naaman's skin was like the skin of a child. He was cured of his leprosy!

Jumping in his chariot, Naaman drove back to Elisha's house, his aides following behind. He hurried into the house and stood before the prophet. "Indeed, now I know that there is no God in all the earth, except in Israel," said Naaman. "Now therefore, please take a gift from your servant."

"As the Lord lives, before whom I stand, I will receive nothing," said Elisha.

Although Naaman urged the prophet to accept his rich presents, he would not take anything. The commander went on his way northward toward home.

Gehazi, Elisha's servant, had listened to all the talk about silver and gold and beautiful robes. His own clothing was shabby and patched. After Naaman had been gone a short while, Gehazi hurried after him. When the Syrian officer saw the man running along the road, he stopped his chariots and went back to meet Elisha's servant. "Is all well?" he asked.

"All is well," said Gehazi. "My master has sent me, saying, 'Indeed, just now two young men of the sons of the prophets have come to me from the mountains of Ephraim. Please give them a talent of silver and two changes of garments.' "

Of course, Gehazi was lying. But Naaman was so happy to be healed of his leprosy that he gave the servant more than he had asked for. "Please, take two talents," said Naaman, heaping the treasure and clothes upon the man.

THOUGHT QUESTION: Why did Elisha ask Naaman to wash in the dirty Jordan River?

Gehazi returned to his house and hid the gifts. Then he went and stood before Elisha. The prophet said, "Where did you go, Gehazi?"

"Your servant did not go anywhere," Gehazi lied.

"Did not my heart go with you when the man turned back from his chariot to meet you?" said the prophet. "Is it time to receive money and to receive clothing, olive groves and vineyards, sheep and oxen, male and female servants? Therefore the leprosy of Naaman shall cling to you and your descendants forever."

So Gehazi left Elisha's presence a leper, as white as snow.

It must have been a day of excitement and happiness when Naaman

> **GOD SAYS:**
>
> "[He] stood before him; and said, 'Indeed, now I know that there is no God in all the earth, except in Israel.'"
>
> –2 Kings 5:15

arrived home. His wife marveled when she saw that her husband was free from the fearful disease. The captive maid must have been overjoyed for her master! Not only had he returned well and strong, but now he worshiped the true God whom she loved. Because this faithful girl had been true to her God in a foreign country, her prayers were answered.

ELISHA CAPTURES AN ARMY

2 Kings 6:8–13:20

The king of Syria decided to make war with Israel. He counseled with his officers on the best secret moves to raid some Israelite towns. However, time after time the army of Syria attempted to ambush soldiers of the Israelite army, only to find that they had escaped. The Syrian king thought that a traitor in his army must be giving military secrets to the enemy. He called his officers together and asked, "Will you not show me which of us is for the king of Israel?"

"None, my Lord, O king," said one of his servants, "but Elisha, the prophet who is in Israel, tells the king of Israel the words you speak in your bedroom."

"Go and see where he is," said the king, "that I may send and get him."

Soon a servant reported back, "He is in Dothan."

Immediately the king of Syria sent a large force of warriors with horses and chariots to surround the city of Dothan. They came swiftly in the night and took up their positions. The next morning when Elisha and his servant woke up, they saw the enemy army all around the city.

"Alas, my master! What shall we do?" Elisha's servant cried.

"Do not fear," said the prophet, "for those who are with us are more than those who are with them." Then Elisha prayed, "Lord, I pray, open his eyes that he may see."

The servant's eyes bugged out when he saw the mountains around the city full of horses and chariots of fire. The Lord had

sent His angels to protect those who trusted in Him.

The Syrian army advanced to capture Elisha. When the soldiers came near, the prophet prayed to God, "Strike this people, I pray, with blindness."

The soldiers became blind and lost. They stood still in the town, not knowing where they were. Elisha came out to meet the army of Syria and said, "This is not the way, nor is this the city. Follow me, and I will bring you to the man whom you seek."

It must have been an amusing sight to see Elisha leading the Syrian army down the road. He guided the soldiers to Samaria, the city of the king of Israel. When they were inside the city, the prophet asked God to open their eyes. Now when the king of Israel saw the helpless enemy army trapped in front of him, he asked the prophet, "My father, shall I kill them? Shall I kill them?" He was anxious to be rid of this threat to his kingdom.

"You shall not kill them," Elisha replied. "Would you kill those whom you have taken captive with your sword and your bow? Set food and water before them, that they may eat and drink and go to their master." Elisha knew that in this case, being kind and fair would produce a better result than killing.

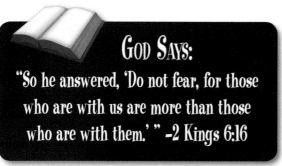

GOD SAYS:

"So he answered, 'Do not fear, for those who are with us are more than those who are with them.' " -2 Kings 6:16

So, the king made a great feast for the army of Syria. When the soldiers had eaten as much as they could, the Israelite ruler sent them home. The soldiers reported to their king the good treatment they had received in Samaria. The two nations became friendly again, and the Syrians did not conduct raids on God's people anymore.

Elisha continued faithfully in his work for the Lord. After

many years, when the prophet was old, he became seriously ill. Joash, the king of Israel at that time, came to visit the prophet. He was troubled because once more the Syrians were striking hard against Israel. With tears in his eyes he said to Elisha, "O my father, my father, the chariots of Israel and their horsemen!" These were the same words Elisha himself had spoken when the prophet Elijah had been taken up to heaven. King Joash had come to get the prophet's counsel in this national crisis.

"Take a bow and some arrows," Elisha said. "Put your hand on the bow."

When the king had a bow and was holding it, Elisha placed his hands on the king's hands. Then the prophet said, "Open the east window."

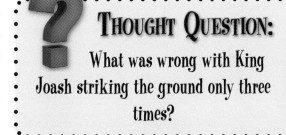

THOUGHT QUESTION:
What was wrong with King Joash striking the ground only three times?

When the window was open, Elisha commanded, "Shoot!"

Joash drew back the bow and let the arrow fly. "The arrow of the Lord's deliverance and the arrow of deliverance from Syria," Elisha exclaimed, "for you must strike the Syrians at Aphek till you have destroyed them."

Elisha had more instructions for the king. "Take the arrows," he said, and King Joash picked them up.

"Strike the ground," the prophet said.

The king struck the ground three times with the arrows. Elisha was angry with Joash. "You should have struck five or six times," he said, "then you would have struck Syria till you had destroyed it! But now you will strike Syria only three times."

Soon after this incident, the old prophet died. Israel had lost a messenger for God who was a kind and faithful judge.

JONAH'S NARROW ESCAPE

Jonah 1–4

F ar to the east of Israel and Syria arose the great empire of Assyria. Its kings were mighty rulers. When they sent out their armies, they conquered the smaller nations. Israel and Judah were now two separate nations with their own kings. When the king of Israel heard about the Assyrians, he was afraid, and rightly so. The day would come when the fierce warriors from Nineveh would attack his capital city of Samaria.

In the little country of Judah, the land of the two tribes of Benjamin and Judah, lived a prophet named Jonah. The Lord sent a message to him. "Arise, go to Nineveh, that great city, and cry out against it; for their wickedness has come up before Me."

The prophet might have been afraid to face the people of the capital city of Assyria, or he might not have wanted to take a long trip to a foreign country. Whatever his reason, Jonah hurried in the opposite direction to Joppa by the sea, instead of heading east for Nineveh. When the man arrived at the seaport, he bought a ticket for a ship sailing to Tarshish, a city far to the west. *Now,* thought Jonah, *I will get away where God cannot find me.*

After the ship had sailed from the harbor to the open sea, the prophet went down into the hold and fell asleep. Soon a terrible windstorm struck the boat. The wind howled, and huge waves crashed over the sides of the vessel. Even the sailors were frightened, and each man called on his pagan gods for help. The storm grew so severe that it seemed the ship would be swamped. In desperation the crew threw the cargo overboard to lighten the ship.

The captain went down into the hold of the ship and found Jonah sound asleep. "What do you mean, sleeper?" asked the captain. "Arise, call on your God; perhaps your God will consider us, so that we may not perish."

The men on board said one to another, "Come, let us cast lots, that we may know for whose cause this trouble has come upon us."

So, they cast lots, which is like throwing dice, and the lot fell on Jonah. They looked at this man who had bought passage on the ship, and they said, "Please tell us! For whose cause is this trouble upon us? What is your occupation? And where do you come from? What is your country? And of what people are you?"

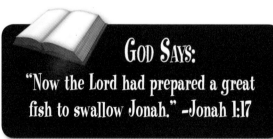

GOD SAYS:
"Now the Lord had prepared a great fish to swallow Jonah." –Jonah 1:17

Jonah told the men that he was a Hebrew and that he had run away from his God-given assignment. He told them that he worshiped the Creator of the sea and the land. When the men heard this, they were terrified and asked, "Why have you done this?"

After talking together, the sailors asked Jonah, "What shall we do to you that the sea may be calm for us?" The windstorm was getting worse by the minute.

"Pick me up," said Jonah, "and throw me into the sea; then the sea will become calm for you. For I know that this great tempest is because of me."

The sailors refused to throw Jonah overboard. They put out the oars and tried to row the ship back toward land. But the heavy waves beat against the ship, and the

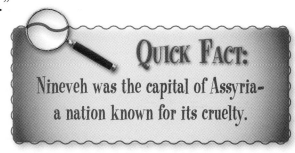

QUICK FACT: Nineveh was the capital of Assyria— a nation known for its cruelty.

storm grew worse. Finally they cried out to the God of heaven in their terror, saying, "We pray, O Lord, please do not let us perish for this man's life, and do not charge us with innocent blood; for You, O Lord, have done as it pleased You."

So, they picked up Jonah and tossed him overboard into the roaring sea. When they had done this, the windstorm died down, and the waves grew calm.

Jonah was trying to keep his head above the waves when "a great fish" came swimming toward him. He must have cried out in fear and terror as the huge mouth of the fish opened. The next thing Jonah knew, he felt himself being sucked into the giant jaws and swallowed! Down, down he went into the belly of the fish. "The Lord had prepared a great fish to swallow Jonah," the Bible says.

For three days and three nights Jonah tossed about in the stomach of the great fish. He must have been panicked and frightened. He knew what was happening, however, and he prayed to God, promising that if he was saved alive he would obey and go to Nineveh to preach.

After three days the fish threw up Jonah on the beach, and the prophet returned to his home, thankful that his life had been spared. Soon the message of the Lord came to Jonah a second time, saying, "Arise, go to Nineveh, that great city, and preach to it the message that I tell you."

This time Jonah did not hesitate. He started for Nineveh immediately. When he reached the great city on the banks of the Tigris River, he went through the streets shouting, "Yet forty days, and Nineveh shall be overthrown!"

The people of Nineveh were sinful and wicked, but when they heard this warning they began to mourn. The king sent out a decree that every person should fast and repent of his sins and call upon God. Very quickly the whole city turned away from evil ways. When the Lord saw that the Assyrians wanted to do right, He determined not to destroy Nineveh.

But when Jonah found out that the city would not be destroyed, he was angry. It seemed to him that his work had been for nothing. He decided that life wasn't worth living, and he prayed, "Therefore now, O Lord, please take my life from me, for it is better for me to die than to live!"

The Lord said, "Is it right for you to be angry?"

Without answering the question, Jonah left the city and walked to where he could look over the big metropolis. He built a shelter for shade because the sun was very warm. The Lord God made a wild gourd vine grow over the shelter to relieve the misery of the angry prophet. Jonah was thankful for the cool shade of the vine.

The prophet stayed in his shelter all night. The next morning, God allowed a worm to eat through the vine so that it quickly withered. Then a hot wind blew, and the sun beat down on Jonah. Again he wished he were dead.

The Lord said, "You have had pity on the plant for which you have not labored, nor made it grow, which came up in a night and perished in a night. And should I not

THOUGHT QUESTION:
Why was Jonah so angry with God for sparing Nineveh?

pity Nineveh, that great city, in which are more than one hundred and twenty thousand persons who cannot discern between their right hand and their left—and much livestock?"

In this way God taught the prophet from Judah that He loves people of all nations and all races. It was a wonderful example of the Father's mercy. God is ready to forgive all who will repent of their sins, if they will turn to Him with all their heart and mind. Jonah learned, too, that he could never run away from the Lord, who sees all that we do and who hears all that we say.

AN ANGEL DESTROYS THE ASSYRIAN ARMY

2 Kings 18–20

Because the people of Nineveh believed the message of Jonah and asked God to forgive their sins, their city was spared. As time went by, the Assyrian Empire grew stronger and conquered other nations.

Young Prince Hezekiah came to the throne of Judah, the little kingdom in the south of Palestine, at a time when Assyria had threatened to attack. When he began to reign at the age of twenty-five, Hezekiah determined to follow the way of the Lord. He destroyed the idols of Baal and opened the temple of the Lord that had been closed for many years. Hezekiah also broke in pieces the bronze serpent that Moses had made to save the people from the plague in the wilderness. Some of the Israelites had offered sacrifices to it and worshiped it during the reign of the evil kings. The Bible says that King Hezekiah "held fast to the Lord; he did not depart from following Him, but kept His commandments, which the Lord had commanded Moses."

When Hezekiah had ruled for four years, the king of Assyria sent his army to attack Samaria, the capital of Israel. Soon the city was captured. Ten years later, Sennacherib, king of Assyria, came against Judah and captured some of its cities. Hezekiah remembered what had happened to Israel, so he wrote a letter to the Assyrian ruler, saying, "I have done wrong; turn away from me; whatever you impose on me I will pay." Sennacherib required Hezekiah to pay three hundred talents of silver and thirty talents of gold as tribute money. This took so much treasure from the little kingdom that King Hezekiah was forced to remove the silver from the temple and strip the gold from the doors and pillars of that beautiful building.

Soon the Assyrian king decided to capture Judah in spite of the tribute money paid to him. He would take the city of Jerusalem. Sennacherib sent his commander in chief to the capital, and with him went a crafty man who held a high office in the Assyrian kingdom. This man did his best to discourage the people of Judah and cause them to surrender. To Hezekiah's officers he said, "Say now to Hezekiah, 'Thus says the great king, the king of Assyria: "What confidence is this in which you trust? You speak of having plans

GOD SAYS:

"He trusted in the Lord God of Israel, so that after him was none like him among all the kings of Judah, nor who were before him." -2 Kings 18:5

and power for war; but they are mere words. And in whom do you trust, that you rebel against me? . . . Have I now come up without the Lord against this place to destroy it? The Lord said to me, 'Go up against this land, and destroy it.' " ' "

The crafty man also spoke to the men of Judah, but they refused to answer. As soon as King Hezekiah heard what the Assyrians were doing, he tore his garments, covered himself with sackcloth, and went to the temple to pray. The king also sent a messenger to the prophet Isaiah, asking him to pray for the nation.

The prophet sent this message of courage back to King Hezekiah, "Thus says the Lord: 'Do not be afraid of the words which you have heard, with which the servants of the king of Assyria have blasphemed Me. Surely I will send a spirit upon him, and he shall hear a rumor and return to his own land; and I will cause him to fall by the sword in his own land.' "

Soon after this, the crafty official returned to the king of Assyria and told him that the men of Judah had refused to surrender. This caused Sennacherib to write an insulting letter to Hezekiah. When the king of Judah received it, he went to the temple and spread the message out before the Lord and prayed, "O Lord God of Israel, the One who dwells between the cherubim, You are God, You alone, of all the kingdoms of the earth. You have made heaven and earth. Incline Your ear, O Lord,

and hear; open Your eyes, O Lord, and see; and hear the words of Sennacherib, which he has sent to reproach the living God. . . . Now therefore, O Lord our God, I pray, save us from his hand, that all the kingdoms of the earth may know that You are the Lord God, You alone."

After Hezekiah prayed, Isaiah the prophet sent him this answer from the Lord: "Thus says the Lord God of Israel: 'Because you have prayed to Me against Sennacherib king of Assyria, I have heard.' . . . .

'He shall not come into this city,
  Nor shoot an arrow there,
  Nor come before it with shield,
  Nor build a siege mound against it.

By the way that he came,
  By the same shall he return;
  And he shall not come into this city,'
Says the Lord."

That night the angel of the Lord went through the army of the Assyrians as it was camped near Jerusalem and killed 185,000 of the enemy. The next morning the people of Judah found the dead lying in the camp. The king of Assyria had gone back to Nineveh, taking with him the handful of men who remained.

The great victory has been described by a famous Victorian poet:

The Assyrian came down like the wolf on the fold,
And his cohorts were gleaming in purple and gold;
And the sheen of their spears was like stars on the
  sea,

When the blue wave rolls nightly on deep Galilee.
Like the leaves of the forest when Summer is
    green,
That host with their banners at sunset were seen:
Like the leaves of the forest when Autumn hath
    blown,
That host on the morrow lay withered and strown.

For the Angel of Death spread his wings on the
    blast,
And breathed in the face of the foe as he passed;
And the eyes of the sleepers waxed deadly and chill,
And their hearts but once heaved, and for ever grew
    still!

And there lay the steed with his nostril all wide,
But through it there rolled not the breath of his
    pride;
And the foam of his gasping lay white on the turf,
And cold as the spray of the rock-beating surf.

And there lay the rider distorted and pale,
With the dew on his brow, and the rust on his
    mail:
And the tents were all silent, the banners alone,
The lances unlifted, the trumpet unblown.

And the widows of Ashur are loud in their wail,
And the idols are broke in the temple of Baal;
And the might of the Gentile, unsmote by the
    sword,
Hath melted like snow in the glance of the Lord!
    (Lord Byron, *The Destruction of Sennacherib*).

The message of God's prophet came true, and Judah was saved from destruction.

Now in those days, Hezekiah took suddenly ill with a severe abscess or boil. Isaiah visited the king and said, "Thus says the Lord: 'Set your house in order, for you shall die, and not live.' "

Hezekiah was heartbroken. He turned his face to the wall and prayed. "Remember now, O Lord, I pray, how I have walked before You in truth and with a loyal heart, and have done what was good in Your sight." And the king wept bitterly.

Isaiah left the king's bedroom; but while he was walking through the courtyard, another message came to him from God. "Return and tell Hezekiah the leader of My people, 'Thus says the Lord, the God of David your father: "I have heard your prayer, I have seen your tears; surely I will heal you. On the third day you shall go up to the house of the Lord. And I will add to your days fifteen years. I will deliver you and this city from the hand of the king of Assyria; and I will defend this city for My own sake, and for the sake of My servant David." ' "

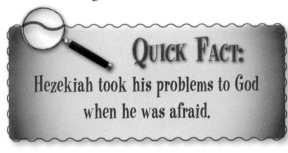

QUICK FACT:
Hezekiah took his problems to God when he was afraid.

Isaiah also gave the king special treatment for the infection. "Take a lump of figs," said the prophet. One of the royal servants laid it on the boil, and Hezekiah recovered.

The king wanted to know for sure that he would get well and live for fifteen more years. He said to Isaiah, "What is the sign that the Lord will heal me, and that I shall go up to the house of the Lord the third day?"

"This is the sign to you from the Lord, that the Lord will do the thing which He has spoken," Isaiah replied. "Shall the shadow go forward ten degrees, or backward ten degrees?"

Hezekiah said, "It is an easy thing for the shadow to go down ten degrees; no, but let the shadow go backward ten degrees."

King Hezekiah watched his sundial carefully. The shadow was moving backward. One, two, five degrees. Then back ten full degrees! Only the God of heaven could move the earth and the sun. The king praised God when he saw the shadow move backward, because he knew that his prayer for more years of life would be answered.

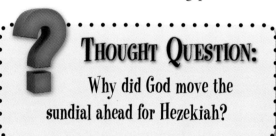

THOUGHT QUESTION:

Why did God move the sundial ahead for Hezekiah?

The king of Babylon in his palace on the Euphrates River heard that Hezekiah had recovered from his serious sickness. The Babylonian ruler sent messengers to Jerusalem with a present for the king of Judah. King Hezekiah was proud to have officers visit him from the far-off empire in the east. He took them into his treasure house and showed them his silver, gold, spices, fine oil, and all his weapons of war.

The king missed a golden opportunity to tell these messengers about the God who created the heavens and the earth. He could have related to them how he had been healed of his illness and how the sun turned back ten degrees. Instead, pride and vanity overtook the king's mind, and the messengers went back to Babylon to tell their sovereign of the riches the little kingdom of Judah possessed.

Isaiah came and stood before Hezekiah and reproved him with a message from God. He said, "Behold, the days are coming when all that is in your house, and what your fathers have accumulated until this day, shall be carried to Babylon; nothing shall be left." The prophet continued, "And they shall take away some of your sons who will descend from you, whom you will beget; and they shall be eunuchs in the palace of the king of Babylon."

"The word of the Lord which you have spoken is good!" said Hezekiah. He was thankful the enemy would not come against Judah during his lifetime.

A Prophet Faces Death

Jeremiah 1–36

Josiah, the great-grandson of Hezekiah, came to the throne of Judah when he was only eight years of age. At the same time, a boy named Jeremiah was growing up in the village of Anathoth, three miles northeast of Jerusalem. This boy would live to see the rise of the Babylonian Empire and the end of Egypt's power. He would also witness the destruction of his own country, for in his lifetime he was to see cruel, ferocious enemies crossing and re-crossing Judah, ravaging the land and destroying its cities.

Jeremiah was a quiet young man of the tribe of Levi, trained like Samuel before him to be a priest. He knew the sad history of his nation after Hezekiah, when the wickedness of King Manasseh and King Amon had caused the people to worship idols. Jeremiah was happy to see the new day when young King Josiah turned the people back to the worship of the true God.

The young king Josiah repaired the neglected temple of the Lord. While the work was going on, Hilkiah the high priest discovered a scroll that contained a copy of the law.

Shaphan the scribe read it to King Josiah, and he was shocked to learn how far the nation had drifted from God. When the scribe had finished reading, Josiah tore his clothes and mourned. Then he gave a command to Hilkiah. "Go, inquire of the Lord for me, for the people and for all Judah, concerning the words of this book that has been found; for great is the wrath of the Lord that is aroused against us, because our fathers have not obeyed the words of this book, to do according to all that is written concerning us."

The king gathered all the elders of the land together, along with the inhabitants of Jerusalem, and he read the words of the law in their hearing. Then he made a covenant with the Lord to obey the commandments. Likewise, all the people pledged themselves to obey God's commands. The altars to pagan gods were broken down, and idol worship was abolished throughout the nation.

GOD SAYS:

" 'Do not say, "I am a youth," for you shall go to all to whom I send you, and whatever I command you, you shall speak.' " –Jeremiah 1:7

In the thirteenth year of King Josiah, God called young Jeremiah to be a prophet. He was given the difficult task of reproving the people for their sins. When called to give the message of repentance, he said, "Ah, Lord God! Behold, I cannot speak, for I am a youth."

But the Lord said, "Do not say, 'I am a youth,' for you shall go to all to whom I send you, and whatever I command you, you shall speak. Do not be afraid of their faces, for I am with you to deliver you."

Then the Lord put His hand to the young man's mouth and touched it. God said, "Behold, I have put My words in your

mouth. See, I have this day set you over the nations and over the kingdoms, to root out and to pull down, to destroy and to throw down, to build and to plant."

Jeremiah was told to go to the cities and talk to the crowds in the marketplaces and in the streets. He must warn them that if they continued in their rebellious ways the nation would be destroyed. The young prophet gave the message, but most of the people refused to listen. Then the Lord described to Jeremiah the doom that was certain to come upon Judah. He was told how a mighty enemy would come down from the north and overthrow the cities and destroy the temple. Because the people would not obey the commands of God, they would be taken into exile as slaves of an enemy king.

Again the nation refused to listen to the warnings. When King Josiah died, many people turned against Jeremiah and called him a traitor because he had warned of trouble to come.

Josiah's son Jehoahaz became king and had reigned only three months when Necho, king of Egypt, came to Jerusalem and took him prisoner. Pharaoh Necho placed Eliakim, another son of Josiah, on the throne and changed his name to Jehoiakim. Pharaoh also ordered the nation of Judah to pay him a huge tribute of silver and gold.

In the middle of this crisis, Jeremiah went to the court of the temple to warn the people of approaching doom. The Lord had told the prophet, "Stand in the court of the Lord's house, and speak to all the cities of Judah, which come to worship in the Lord's house, all the words that I command you to speak to them. Do not diminish a word. Perhaps everyone will listen and turn from his evil way, that I may relent concerning the calamity which I purpose to bring on them because of the evil of their doings."

When the priests and prophets heard the words that Jeremiah spoke, they became angry. After he had finished speaking, they grabbed him and said, "You will surely die! Why have you prophesied in the name of the Lord, saying, 'This house shall be like Shiloh, and this city shall be desolate, without an inhabitant'?"

Soon a mob crowded around Jeremiah. When the princes of Judah heard what was happening, they came from the palace and took their seats at the new gate at the entrance of the temple. The priests and prophets called out to the rulers, saying, "This man deserves to die! For he has prophesied against this city, as you have heard with your ears."

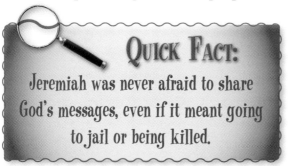

QUICK FACT:
Jeremiah was never afraid to share God's messages, even if it meant going to jail or being killed.

While the angry mob shouted for Jeremiah's death, the prophet never flinched from his duty. He turned to the princes and made a bold appeal. He said, "The Lord sent me to prophesy against this house and against this city with all the words that you have heard. Now therefore, amend your ways and your doings, and obey the voice of the Lord your God; then the Lord will relent concerning the doom that He has pronounced against you. As for me, here I am, in your hand; do with me as seems good and proper to you. But know for certain that if you put me to death, you will surely bring innocent blood on yourselves, on this city, and on its inhabitants; for truly the Lord has sent me to you to speak all these words in your hearing."

A silence fell on the crowd. Then the princes and all the people said to the priests, "This man does not deserve to die. For he has spoken to us in the name of the Lord our God." At that moment the angry crowd sided with Jeremiah, and he was saved from death.

Some of the elders came forward and spoke to the people. They reminded them that in the days of King Hezekiah, a prophet of the Lord had given severe messages to the nation, but he had not been put to death. "Did Hezekiah king of Judah and all Judah ever put him to death?" they asked. "Did he not fear the Lord and seek the Lord's favor? And the Lord relented concerning the doom which He had pronounced against them. But we are doing great evil against ourselves."

While Jeremiah was saved, another prophet named Urijah, who prophesied the same message from the Lord, did not escape the anger of the king. Although this second prophet escaped to Egypt, officers of Jehoiakim followed him and brought him back to Jerusalem. King Jehoiakim killed Urijah with a sword.

Friends of Jeremiah saved him in his time of danger. Ahikam, a close friend of Jeremiah's, gave shelter to the prophet and protected him from the people who wanted to kill him.

Although Jeremiah's enemies were unable to get to him, they put so much pressure on the government authorities that at last the prophet was imprisoned and placed in stocks. Even in the dungeon Jeremiah did not give up the task of speaking God's message. He said,

But His word was in my heart like a burning fire
Shut up in my bones;
I was weary of holding it back,
And I could not.

The time came when the Lord told Jeremiah to write down on a scroll every warning he had been given for Judah. The prophet called Baruch, a young friend who acted as his secretary, and dictated the messages to him. Then Jeremiah said to Baruch, "You go, therefore, and read from the scroll which you have written at my instruction, the words of the Lord, in the hearing of the people in the Lord's house on the day of fasting. And you shall also read them in the hearing of all

Judah who come from their cities. It may be that they will present their supplication before the Lord, and everyone will turn from his evil way. For great is the anger and the fury that the Lord has pronounced against this people."

Baruch followed the instructions of Jeremiah. The day of fasting came, when the temple was filled with people. Standing at the window of a second-floor room, he read the words of the Lord in the hearing of all the people. Now Michaiah, the grandson of Shaphan, saw what was happening and hurried off to the palace to tell the princes about Baruch.

The princes immediately sent a messenger to bring Baruch and the scroll to the palace. Baruch came before the king's officers and read to them from the scroll as he was commanded. When the officers heard the words of Jeremiah, they were afraid and said, "We will surely tell the king of all these words."

Then they asked Baruch, "Tell us now, how did you write all these words—at his instruction?"

"He proclaimed with his mouth all these words to me, and I wrote them with ink in the book," Baruch answered.

"Go and hide, you and Jeremiah," the princes said, "and let no one know where you are."

Baruch hurried away, leaving the scroll with the king's officers. They reported the matter to King Jehoiakim. Jehudi the scribe read Jeremiah's message from the scroll. The king was living in his winter house at that time. He was sitting near a fire that was burning on the hearth. As Jehudi read each portion of the scroll, the king cut it off with the scribe's knife and tossed it into the flames. Part by part, God's message was thrown into the fire and consumed.

Three of the scribes begged the king not to burn the scroll. But King Jehoiakim and his wicked followers were not afraid of the divine warnings. They did not repent of their sins. After the message had been read, the king ordered the arrest of Baruch the secretary and Jeremiah the prophet. But God had hidden them.

The Lord gave more instructions to the prophet Jeremiah. "Take yet another scroll, and write on it all the former words that were in the first scroll which Jehoiakim the king of Judah has burned."

THOUGHT QUESTION: Why wouldn't the people listen to Jeremiah's warnings?

In this second message Jeremiah gave more warnings of disaster that would come to the evil king and the whole nation. In this way the Lord tried again to turn the people of Judah from their disobedience. He wanted to save them from destruction at the hand of their enemies. But they would not listen to the warnings.

JERUSALEM FALLS TO THE ARMY OF BABYLON

Jeremiah 37–52

The day came, as Jeremiah had predicted, when Nebuchadnezzar, king of Babylon, sent his armies against Judah. He forced King Jehoiakim to pay tribute as a vassal king. After three years of this bondage, King Jehoiakim thought that he was strong enough to rebel against the Babylonian king, but his plans failed. Soon Jehoiakim died, and his eighteen-year-old son, Jehoiachin, came to the throne. The young king had reigned only three months, however, when Nebuchadnezzar came to Jerusalem with a stronger army and captured it.

When King Jehoiachin surrendered, it was a sorry day for the royal family. The king's mother, his wives, his nobles, and his officers became captives of Nebuchadnezzar. They and ten thousand Jewish soldiers and many of the best people of Judah were carried away to the city of Babylon. King Nebuchadnezzar made King Jehoiachin's uncle, Zedekiah, ruler of the captive kingdom.

About this time the Babylonian, or Chaldean, army withdrew from the city of Jerusalem. They feared the armies of Egypt that were advancing from the south. At this time Jeremiah the prophet attempted to leave Jerusalem. He wanted to visit his property in the land of Benjamin. At the city gate a captain of the guard challenged him.

"You are defecting to the Chaldeans!" the captain said loudly.

"False! I am not defecting to the Chaldeans," Jeremiah responded.

But the captain would not listen to Jeremiah. He arrested him and brought him before the princes of Judah. The princes were angry with the prophet and beat him. They put him in prison, and he remained there many days. While he was in prison, the Chaldean army returned and surrounded Jerusalem. King Zedekiah sent for Jeremiah and asked him secretly, "Is there any word from the Lord?"

"There is," answered Jeremiah. "You shall be delivered into the hand of the king of Babylon!"

Jeremiah then asked the king not to send him back to prison. Zedekiah decided to send Jeremiah to the court of the prison rather than a prison cell, and ordered that the prophet be given a loaf of bread each day as long as there was any food in the city. Since the Chaldean army had surrounded the city, food was becoming scarce.

QUICK FACT:

Jeremiah warned the king not to rebel against Babylon or he would lose the land.

The situation grew worse as famine and disease broke out among the people. Jeremiah warned the citizens, "Thus says the Lord: 'He who remains in this city shall die by the sword, by famine, and by pestilence; but he who goes over to the Chaldeans shall live; his life shall be as a prize to him, and he shall live.' Thus says the Lord: 'This city shall surely be given into the hand of the king of

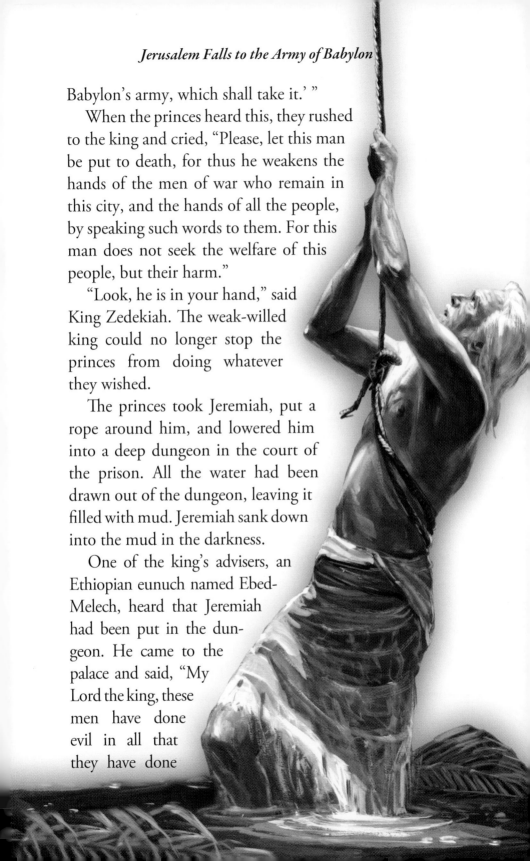

Babylon's army, which shall take it.' "

When the princes heard this, they rushed to the king and cried, "Please, let this man be put to death, for thus he weakens the hands of the men of war who remain in this city, and the hands of all the people, by speaking such words to them. For this man does not seek the welfare of this people, but their harm."

"Look, he is in your hand," said King Zedekiah. The weak-willed king could no longer stop the princes from doing whatever they wished.

The princes took Jeremiah, put a rope around him, and lowered him into a deep dungeon in the court of the prison. All the water had been drawn out of the dungeon, leaving it filled with mud. Jeremiah sank down into the mud in the darkness.

One of the king's advisers, an Ethiopian eunuch named Ebed-Melech, heard that Jeremiah had been put in the dungeon. He came to the palace and said, "My Lord the king, these men have done evil in all that they have done to Jeremiah the prophet, whom they have cast into the dungeon, and he is likely to die from hunger in the place where he is."

The king must have agreed with his adviser, because he said, "Take from here thirty men with you, and lift Jeremiah the prophet out of the dungeon before he dies." Ebed-Melech and the thirty men found some old clothes and rags and went to the dungeon. They tied the rags to some ropes and let them down to Jeremiah.

"Please put these old clothes and rags under your armpits, under the ropes," Ebed-Melech called down to the prophet.

Jeremiah did so, and the men pulled him up out of the filth in the dungeon.

Once more King Zedekiah sent for Jeremiah and asked him to tell the truth concerning the future of the country. Jeremiah said to the king, "If I declare it to you, will you not surely put me to death?"

King Zedekiah swore an oath in secret that he would protect the prophet from those who wished to do him harm. Then Jeremiah made a final appeal to the king to end the siege.

"If you surely surrender to the king of Babylon's princes, then your soul shall live; this city shall not be burned with fire, and you and your house shall live. But if you do not surrender to the king of Babylon's princes, then this city shall be given into the hand of the Chaldeans; they shall burn it with fire, and you shall not escape from their hand."

The king was weak, however. He could not stand up to the princes, and he refused to surrender. The enemy army made a final fierce attack. They broke down the walls of the city, and the soldiers swarmed into the palace. King Zedekiah tried to run away but was captured. His two sons were killed, and the king was blinded and taken in chains to Babylon. He remained a prisoner there until he died.

Before the Chaldean army left Jerusalem, they burned down Solomon's temple and the king's palace. Many of the other beautiful buildings in the city were destroyed.

The Babylonian captain in command of the city, Nebuzaradan, treated Jeremiah kindly. He released the prophet from the court of the prison and said to him, "Now look, I free you this day from the chains that were on your hand. If it seems good to you to come with me to Babylon, come, and I will look after you. But if it seems wrong for you to come with me to Babylon, remain here. See, all the land is before you; wherever it seems good and convenient for you to go, go there." Jeremiah decided to stay in the land of Judah. He lived among the poor people who had been left behind at the time the Chaldeans took captives from Jerusalem.

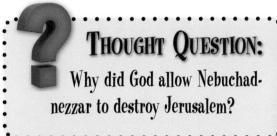

THOUGHT QUESTION: Why did God allow Nebuchadnezzar to destroy Jerusalem?

A dispute broke out between ambitious men in Judah and the King of Ammon, who lived beyond the Jordan River. The situation became so desperate that many of the Jews who remained in Judah decided to seek refuge in Egypt. Jeremiah asked the Lord for instruction, and the word came to him that they should not go to Egypt. However, the people refused to accept his message. A large caravan of people and animals set out toward the land of the Nile. They forced Jeremiah and Baruch to go with them.

Through more than forty years Jeremiah was a faithful prophet of God. Although his messages were hated and scorned, although the kings and people refused to obey the word of the Lord, this courageous man stood true and loyal in every crisis. The word of the Lord was in him like a burning fire. He could not be silent when he had a message to give.

THE KING WHO FORGOT HIS DREAM

Daniel 1; 2

Ⱥ ll of the predictions that Isaiah and Jeremiah made concerning the fall of Jerusalem came to pass. In the last
years of the kingdom of Judah the rulers were weak, evil men
who disobeyed the law of the Lord. Finally, Nebuchadnezzar,
king of Babylon, came with his army and captured Jerusalem.
The city was left in ruins and the soldiers marched thousands
of citizens away as prisoners.

Among the captives taken to Babylon from Judah were four
young men of the royal family. They were strong and handsome and capable of learning. Daniel was the young man who
seems to have been the leader of the group. He and his three
companions were taken to the royal palace at Babylon. King
Nebuchadnezzar changed Daniel's name to Belteshazzar, and
his three friends were given the names Shadrach, Meshach,
and Abednego.

These young men had grown up in Judean homes where
they were taught about the true God. They had often gone to
Solomon's temple to worship the Lord who made heaven and
earth. Now they found themselves captives in a country where

pagan idols were worshiped and strange rites and ceremonies performed. The four young princes determined that they would be true to God in every test they faced.

The first problem that came to them was about food. Ashpenaz, the king's officer in charge of the four Hebrews, brought them food and wine from the king's table. Now, the young men had been taught to eat food that was clean according to the Law of Moses. They knew also that some of this food had been offered to

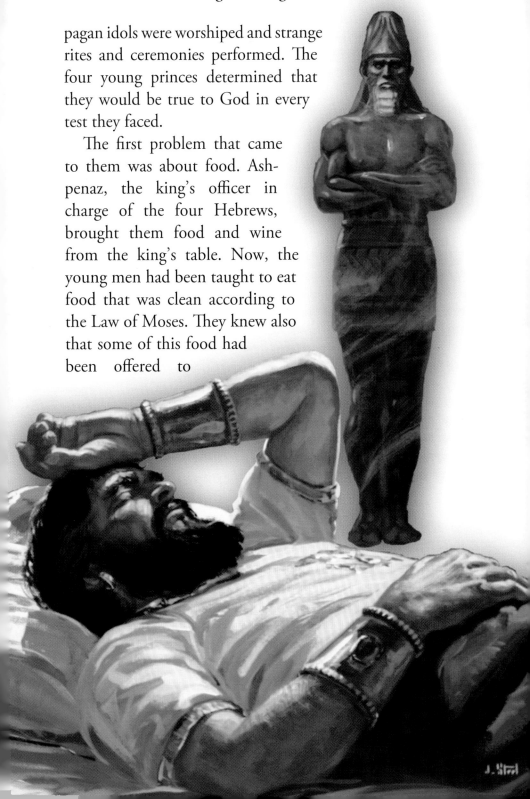

idols. To eat it would mean that they were honoring heathen gods.

Ashpenaz liked Daniel, and when the young prince came to the officer with a request not to be served the king's food or wine, the man listened carefully. Then he said to Daniel, "I fear my Lord the king, who has appointed your food and drink. For why should he see your faces looking worse than the young men who are your age? Then you would endanger my head before the king."

"Please test your servants for ten days," Daniel asked, "and let them give us vegetables to eat and water to drink. Then let our appearance be examined before you, and the appearance of the young men who eat the portion of the king's delicacies; and as you see fit, so deal with your servants."

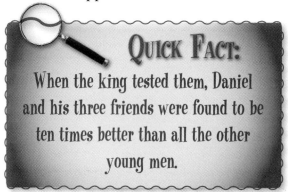

QUICK FACT:
When the king tested them, Daniel and his three friends were found to be ten times better than all the other young men.

The officer agreed to the test, and he allowed the young men to eat simple, healthy food. At the end of ten days they looked better and fatter in appearance than the young men who ate the food of the king. After that the officer allowed the four princes to have a simple diet of vegetables and water for their meals.

Daniel and his companions received training in the king's school. In the examination at the end of their study, they were found to be wiser than even the magicians and astrologers of Babylon.

One night King Nebuchadnezzar had a dream. When he woke up he could not remember his dream, and he was perplexed. He commanded his magicians and enchanters to stand before him and describe what he had dreamed.

"O king, live forever! Tell your servants the dream, and we will give the interpretation," the wise men said.

But the king could not remember his dream. He said, "My decision is firm: if you do not make known the dream to me, and its interpretation, you shall be cut in pieces, and your houses shall be made an ash heap. However, if you tell the dream and its interpretation, you shall receive from me gifts, rewards, and great honor. Therefore tell me the dream and its interpretation."

Again the wise men asked the king to describe his dream, and

GOD SAYS:

" 'He gives wisdom to the wise and knowledge to those who have understanding.' " -Daniel 2:21

then they would give him the meaning of it. Nebuchadnezzar accused them of stalling to gain some time. The magicians realized that they were in a hopeless position.

"There is not a man on earth who can tell the king's matter," they said. "Therefore no king, Lord, or ruler has ever asked such things of any magician, astrologer, or Chaldean. It is a difficult thing that the king requests, and there is no other who can tell it to the king except the gods, whose dwelling is not with flesh."

King Nebuchadnezzar was furious. He commanded that all the wise men of Babylon be killed. This meant that Daniel and his three friends would die, because they were classified as wise men.

Daniel and his companions had not been called to the palace with the other wise men to interpret the king's dream. When Captain Arioch and his soldiers came to kill them, Daniel

asked, "Why is the decree from the king so urgent?"

Arioch explained the reason. Daniel went immediately to the king and asked for more time so that he might tell him the dream and its meaning.

With the king's agreement, Daniel hurried home and told Shadrach, Meshach, and Abednego that they needed to pray. That night, God revealed the dream to Daniel.

The next morning Daniel went to Arioch, the captain of the guard, and pleaded with him not to kill any of the wise men. "Take me before the king," he said, "and I will tell the king the interpretation."

The officer hurried with Daniel to the palace and told King Nebuchadnezzar that he had found a man, one of the captives from Judah, who could reveal the forgotten dream.

"Are you able to make known to me the dream which I have seen, and its interpretation?" the king asked.

Daniel avoided taking honor to himself and humbly replied, "The secret which the king has demanded, the wise men, the astrologers, the magicians, and the soothsayers cannot declare to the king. But there is a God in heaven who reveals secrets, and He has made known to King Nebuchadnezzar what will be in the latter days."

Daniel went on, "You, O king, were watching; and behold, a great image! This great image, whose splendor was excellent, stood before you. . . . This image's head was of fine gold, its chest and arms of silver, its belly and thighs of bronze, its legs of iron, its feet partly of iron and partly of clay. You watched while a stone was cut out without hands, which struck the image on its feet of iron and clay, and broke them in pieces. Then the iron, the clay, the bronze, the silver, and the gold were crushed together, and became like chaff from the summer threshing floors; the wind carried them away so that no trace of them was found. And the stone that struck the image became a great mountain and filled the whole earth.

"This is the dream," Daniel said. "Now we will tell the interpretation of it before the king. You, O king, are a king of kings. For the God of heaven has given you a kingdom, power, strength, and glory; . . . He . . . has made you ruler over . . . all—you are this head of gold."

Daniel explained that after Babylon would come a lesser kingdom, and a third and fourth one after that. Today, because we know the chain of events in history, we know that the silver chest of the image represented Media-Persia, the brass waist was Greece, and the iron legs represented the empire of Rome. The feet of the statue, a mixture of iron and clay, stand for the divided nations in Europe as they are right now. Daniel prophesied that at the end of the days of iron and clay, "the God of heaven will set up a kingdom which shall never be destroyed; and the kingdom shall not be left to other people."

THOUGHT QUESTION:
Why was Nebuchadnezzar given the dream about the statue?

The king was convinced that Daniel had spoken the truth. He came down from his throne and bowed low in front of the young Hebrew. He said, "Truly your God is the God of gods, the Lord of kings, and a revealer of secrets, since you could reveal this secret."

King Nebuchadnezzar made Daniel the governor of the province of Babylon and chief of all the wise men in the empire. And the lives of the other wise men were spared because of Daniel's faithfulness to God.

A FIERY FURNACE AND AN INSANE KING

Daniel 3; 4

K ing Nebuchadnezzar remembered his dream of the great metal image, but he was not satisfied. He didn't want Babylon to be just the head of gold; he wanted his empire to stand forever. He ordered the creation of a giant statue more than a hundred feet tall to be set up on the plain of Dura. It was covered entirely with gold. This image was no doubt meant to show the king's desire to challenge the prophecy that Babylon would someday fall.

The ruler sent for all his governors, judges, counselors, and other high officials to come from all the provinces for the dedication of the golden statue. On the day set for the celebration, a vast multitude of people assembled on the plain of Dura. The herald shouted King Nebuchadnezzar's instructions to the crowd, saying, "To you it is commanded, O peoples, nations, and languages, that at the time you hear the sound of the horn, flute, harp, lyre, and psaltery, in symphony with all kinds of music, you shall fall down and worship the gold image that King Nebuchadnezzar has set up; and whoever does not fall down and worship shall be cast immediately into the midst of a burning fiery furnace."

As soon as the music began to play, all the people of every nation and language bowed before the golden statue, as the king had commanded.

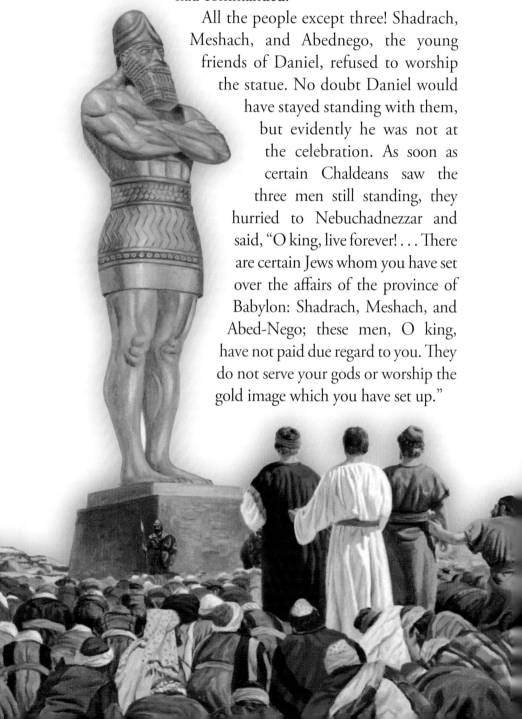

All the people except three! Shadrach, Meshach, and Abednego, the young friends of Daniel, refused to worship the statue. No doubt Daniel would have stayed standing with them, but evidently he was not at the celebration. As soon as certain Chaldeans saw the three men still standing, they hurried to Nebuchadnezzar and said, "O king, live forever! . . . There are certain Jews whom you have set over the affairs of the province of Babylon: Shadrach, Meshach, and Abed-Nego; these men, O king, have not paid due regard to you. They do not serve your gods or worship the gold image which you have set up."

The king became angry. He commanded that the three Hebrews be brought to him, and with fury in his eyes he said, "Is it true, Shadrach, Meshach, and Abed-Nego, that you do not serve my gods or worship the gold image which I have set up?" Nebuchadnezzar said that he would give them another chance. But if they did not bow down as he had commanded, he would have them thrown into the furnace of fire.

"O Nebuchadnezzar, we have no need to answer you in this matter," the young officials said. "If that is the case, our God whom we serve is able to deliver us from the burning fiery furnace, and He will deliver us from your hand, O king. But if not, let it be known to you, O king, that we do not serve your gods, nor will we worship the gold image which you have set up."

When Nebuchadnezzar heard this straightforward reply, the expression on his face changed. He was filled with rage against the three princes who refused to bow at his command. He ordered the furnace to be heated seven times hotter than usual. Then he commanded some of his strongest soldiers to bind the three young men and throw them into the super-heated furnace. The three Hebrews fell down in the middle of the fire. The furnace was so hot that the soldiers who threw the men into the fire were killed by the terrible heat.

King Nebuchadnezzar watched for a moment, and then he became alarmed. He called his ministers and asked, "Did we not cast three men bound into the midst of the fire?"

GOD SAYS:
" 'Our God whom we serve is able to deliver us from the burning fiery furnace.' " –Daniel 3:17

"True, O king," they answered.

"Look!" he said, "I see four men loose, walking in the midst of the fire; and they are not hurt, and the form of the fourth is like the Son of God."

Then King Nebuchadnezzar edged close to the furnace and called out, "Shadrach, Meshach, and Abed-Nego, servants of the Most High God, come out, and come here."

The three men walked out of the furnace, and the amazed officials and the king gathered around. They saw that the fire had not burned them or even singed their hair. There was not even the smell of fire on their clothing!

QUICK FACT:

When Nebuchadnezzar realized the young men weren't hurt, he praised them for their courage and their God.

King Nebuchadnezzar was ready to give the God of heaven praise for protecting the three young men. "Blessed be the God of Shadrach, Meshach, and Abed-Nego, who sent His Angel and delivered His servants who trusted in Him, and they have frustrated the king's word, and yielded their bodies, that they should not serve nor worship any god except their own God!" He made a decree that anyone in the entire kingdom who said anything bad about the God of these three men would be executed and their homes destroyed.

Then the king promoted Shadrach, Meshach, and Abed-nego and gave them more responsibility in the kingdom.

Nebuchadnezzar was so impressed by the power of God in caring for His people that he sent a message to all the people of his kingdom. It said,

"Peace be multiplied to you.

I thought it good to declare the signs and wonders that the Most High God has worked for me.

How great are His signs,
And how mighty His wonders!
His kingdom is an everlasting kingdom,
And His dominion is from generation to generation."

Some time later Nebuchadnezzar had another dream, and he summoned Daniel to reveal its meaning. The king said he saw a giant tree. It was so tall and its branches were so widespread that the animals of the field rested in its shade and the birds rested in its branches.

While the king watched the tree in his dream, he heard a voice from heaven saying,

" 'Chop down the tree and cut off its branches,
Strip off its leaves and scatter its fruit.
Let the beasts get out from under it,
And the birds from its branches.
Nevertheless leave the stump and roots in the earth,
Bound with a band of iron and bronze,
In the tender grass of the field.
Let it be wet with the dew of heaven,
And let him graze with the beasts
On the grass of the earth.
Let his heart be changed from that of a man,
Let him be given the heart of a beast,
And let seven times pass over him.' "

When Daniel heard the dream, he was stunned. He did not know what to say. The king saw the perplexed look on his face and said, "Belteshazzar, do not let the dream or its interpretation trouble you."

"My Lord," Daniel replied, "may the dream concern those who hate you, and its interpretation concern your enemies!

"The tree that you saw, which grew and became strong, whose height reached to the heavens and which could be seen by all the earth, whose leaves were lovely and its fruit abundant, in which was food for all, under which the beasts of the field dwelt, and in whose branches the birds of the heaven had their home—it is you, O king, who have grown and become strong; for your greatness has grown and reaches to the heavens, and your dominion to the end of the earth."

Daniel went on to say that in the same way the huge tree was cut down, so the king would be cut down by losing his mind. In his madness he would be sent out into the fields and eat grass like a cow. For seven years he would be in this state of insanity.

Daniel pleaded with Nebuchadnezzar, "O king, let my advice be acceptable to you; break off your sins by being righteous, and your iniquities by showing mercy to the poor. Perhaps there may be a lengthening of your prosperity."

A year later the king was walking around his palace surveying the great city of many wonders. He said out loud, "Is not this great Babylon, that I have built for a royal dwelling by my mighty power and for the honor of my majesty?"

While he was still speaking, a voice came from heaven saying, "King Nebuchadnezzar, to you it is spoken: the kingdom has departed from you!" That very hour he became insane, and he was driven out into the fields to live like an animal. He ate grass, and his hair grew ragged and long.

When seven years had passed, the king's reasoning power returned. He came back to the royal palace, and his wise men and officials accepted him. They restored him as king over Babylon. Nebuchadnezzar blessed the God of heaven and said,

> For His dominion is an everlasting dominion,
> And His kingdom is from generation to generation.

DANIEL IN THE DEN OF LIONS

Daniel 5; 6

King Nebuchadnezzar died, but the kingdom of Babylon continued in power and greatness. Belshazzar, the grandson of Nebuchadnezzar, was placed in authority in the capital city. This weak man was foolish; he loved only pleasure and glory. Soon his nation faced grave danger. The armies of the Medes and the Persians came against Babylon.

Belshazzar did not worry about the enemy. He thought the strong walls of the city would make it impossible for any enemy to enter. He made a great feast and invited a thousand Lords and nobles to attend. Princes and statesmen came and drank wine and praised their gods of silver and gold.

Amid the feasting, the fingers of a man's hand appeared and began to write on the wall by a lampstand. A hush fell over the royal banquet hall. The king turned pale, and his knees knocked together. He shouted for his astrologers and soothsayers to come. "Whoever reads this writing, and tells me its interpretation," the king said to them, "shall be clothed with purple and have a chain of gold around his neck; and he shall be the third ruler in the kingdom."

All the wise men who entered the banquet hall and saw the writing on the wall could not read it. The queen mother heard the noise of Belshazzar and his Lords, and she came into the hall. She remembered that Daniel had interpreted dreams for King Nebuchadnezzar many years before. "Let Daniel be called," she advised her son, "and he will give the interpretation."

Daniel was hurriedly brought in before the king. When Belshazzar saw the aging prophet he said, "Are you that Daniel who is one of the captives from Judah, whom my father the king brought from Judah? I have heard of you, that the Spirit of God is in you, and that light and understanding and excellent wisdom are found in you. Now the wise men, the astrologers, have been brought in before me, that they should read this writing and make known to me its interpretation, but they could not give the interpretation of the thing. . . . Now if you can read the writing and make known to me its interpretation, you shall be clothed with purple and have a chain of gold around your neck, and shall be the third ruler in the kingdom."

"Let your gifts be for yourself, and give your rewards to another," Daniel said bluntly. "Yet I will read the writing to the king, and make known to him the interpretation."

Daniel then reminded Belshazzar of Nebuchadnezzar mistake in forgetting God and the terrible punishment that came

God Says:

" 'You have been weighed in the balances, and found wanting.' "
–Daniel 5:27

on him. "But you his son, Belshazzar, have not humbled your heart, although you knew all this. And you have lifted yourself up against the Lord of heaven."

Turning to the writing on the wall, Daniel translated the

words. "MENE: God has numbered your kingdom, and finished it; TEKEL: You have been weighed in the balances, and found wanting; PERES: Your kingdom has been divided, and given to the Medes and Persians."

True to his word, Belshazzar had Daniel clothed in purple, a gold chain placed around his neck, and proclaimed him the third ruler in the kingdom. But that very night the army of the Medes and Persians entered the city, overcame the guards, and killed Belshazzar, king of Babylon.

Darius the Mede became king and took over the empire. Daniel continued to serve in the court. King Darius made Daniel one of the three chiefs of his 120 governors. Daniel distinguished himself as honest and wise, so the king considered setting him over the whole kingdom. Of course, some of the officials around him were jealous, and they plotted how they might get Daniel into trouble. But try as they might, they could find no fault with him. The jealous plotters discussed among themselves and concluded, "We shall not find any charge against this Daniel unless we find it against him concerning the law of his God."

With an evil plan laid out, the officials went to the king. They said, "King Darius, live forever! All the governors of the kingdom, the administrators and satraps, the counselors and advisors, have consulted together to establish a royal statute and to make a firm decree, that whoever petitions any god or man for thirty days, except you, O king, shall be cast into the den of lions. Now, O king, establish the decree and sign the writing, so that it cannot be changed, according to the law of the Medes and Persians, which does not alter."

These men knew that Daniel prayed only to the God of heaven. They did not mention this to the king, however. They knew that if he realized how the law would endanger Daniel's life, he would not sign the decree. King Darius was foolishly

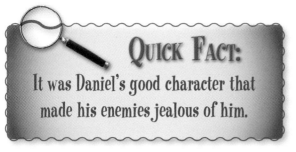

QUICK FACT:
It was Daniel's good character that made his enemies jealous of him.

pleased with the decree and signed it.

When Daniel, the prophet of God, heard about the decree, he went to his house. Every day, three times a day, Daniel opened his windows toward Jerusalem. Then he would kneel and give thanks to the Lord. On this day Daniel prayed as he always had.

His enemies rushed to the house and found Daniel in the act of praying to God. They hurried back to the palace and came before the king.

"Have you not signed a decree," they asked, trying to act natural, "that every man who petitions any god or man within thirty days, except you, O king, shall be cast into the den of lions?"

"The thing is true, according to the law of the Medes and Persians, which does not alter," the king said.

"That Daniel, who is one of the captives from Judah, does not show due regard for you, O king, or for the decree that you have signed, but makes his petition three times a day."

When King Darius heard this, he was extremely upset with himself. Immediately he set his heart on saving Daniel. All day the king worked to find a solution to deliver his faithful governor. At sunset the crafty officials approached King Darius and said, "Know, O king, that it is the law of the Medes and Persians that no decree or statute which the king establishes may be changed."

The king gave the order, and Daniel was thrown into the underground den of lions. King Darius came out to the den and called down to Daniel, "Your God, whom you serve continually, He will deliver you." Then the entrance of the den was covered with a large stone. The king sealed it in wax with his signet ring.

That night the king did not eat. He could not sleep. His thoughts were on Daniel in the den of snarling lions. In the morning, as soon as it was light, King Darius hurried to the den and called in a sad voice, "Daniel, servant of the living God, whom you serve continually, been able to deliver you from the lions?"

The king listened.

"O king, live forever!" Daniel called back. "My God sent His angel and shut the lions' mouths, so that they have not hurt me, because I was found innocent before Him; and also, O king, I have done no wrong before you."

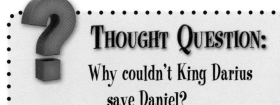

THOUGHT QUESTION:
Why couldn't King Darius save Daniel?

The king was very happy! He ordered servants to pull his friend Daniel from the lions' den. Soon Daniel was standing on the ground again, and he had no injuries at all, not even a scratch!

Darius then commanded that all the men who had accused Daniel should be brought to the lions' den. The wicked officials, with their wives and children, were thrown down to the lions. These lions were ferocious, and they broke the bones of the people before they even hit the bottom of the den.

Then Darius wrote this decree to all nations:

Peace be multiplied to you.

I make a decree that in every dominion of my kingdom men must tremble and fear before the God of Daniel.

Daniel the aging prophet continued to prosper during the reign of Darius, and he was loyal to God all the days of his life.

ESTHER, QUEEN OF GREAT COURAGE

Esther 1–10

Cyrus followed Darius as ruler of the Medo-Persian Empire. When he came to the throne, he decreed that the Hebrews scattered through the provinces of Media-Persia could go back to their homes in Canaan. Thousands returned home, but some stayed where they were. Among those who stayed in Persia was Mordecai, a man of the tribe of Benjamin. He was an officer of the king, and in his house at Shushan lived Esther, his cousin. When Esther was a little girl, her father and mother had died. Mordecai had cared for her as he would his own daughter.

King Xerxes became the ruler of the Persian Empire at this time. In the Bible he is called King Ahasuerus. As he sat in his palace at Shushan, Xerxes decided to make a seven-day feast for all the men of the city. According to the custom of the country, men and women did not eat together at a banquet. Therefore, Queen Vashti would hold a special dinner for the women.

On the last day of the feast, King Xerxes commanded the queen to come to him so that his officials and all the people could see her great beauty. But Queen Vashti refused to go. The king was furious because the queen had disobeyed him in front of the nobles and officials. So, he ruled that she would no longer be his queen.

Later, when the king's anger had died down, he decided to choose a new queen from among the beautiful maidens of the empire. Messengers went around all the provinces to bring maidens to appear at the king's palace. Esther, the cousin of Mordecai, was taken to the palace with the other girls. After twelve months of preparation, each girl was presented to the king. Xerxes liked Esther more than all the other young women, and he chose her to be his queen.

QUICK FACT: The Persians worshiped their gods through their rulers, which is why Mordecai wouldn't bow down to Haman.

As an officer of the king, Mordecai sat at the palace gate. One day he overheard the plot of two angry servants. They were upset with King Xerxes and were making plans to kill him. Mordecai sent a message to Queen Esther, and she told the king. The men were soon discovered in their treachery and hanged. The details of the incident were written down in the official record of royal business.

About this time, Haman, a proud prince of the court, was promoted to be above all the other princes. The king commanded that all the officials and servants should bow to him. Mordecai did not bow to Haman, because he had been taught to worship God alone. When the servants at the gate saw that Mordecai refused to bow, they told Haman. The chief prince was filled with rage. What could he do? Soon Haman decided on an evil plan. He would do more than punish Mordecai alone.

Haman approached King Xerxes and said, "There is a certain people scattered and dispersed among the people in all the provinces of your kingdom; their laws are different from all other people's, and they do not keep the king's laws. Therefore it is not fitting for the king to let them remain. If it pleases the king, let a decree be written that they be destroyed, and I will pay ten thousand talents of silver into the hands of those who do the work, to bring it into the king's treasuries."

Since the monarch did not know Haman's real purpose, he handed him the royal signet ring and said, "The money and the people are given to you, to do with them as seems good to you." King Xerxes still did not know that his beautiful queen was a Jew.

Haman called a scribe to write the letter commanding the people to kill all the Jews on a certain day. Then messengers carried the letters, sealed with the king's ring, to all the empire. The king and Haman sat down to a drink.

When Mordecai heard about the decree, he tore his clothes and mourned deeply. He knew that this law doomed his people to destruction. As the decree reached Jews living in different parts of the empire, they began to weep. Many of them put on sackcloth and ashes and fasted and prayed.

Queen Esther's maids told her about Mordecai. She sent new clothes to him, but he would not accept them. Esther then sent a eunuch to her cousin to find out the reason for his distress. The servant returned to the queen with a copy of the decree for the destruction of the Jews. He also gave Queen Esther a message from Mordecai saying that she must go to the king and beg for the lives of her people.

Esther sent her servant with this message for Mordecai: "All the king's servants and the people of the king's provinces know that any man or woman who goes into the inner court to the king, who has not been called, he has but one law: put all to death, except the one to whom the king holds out the golden scepter, that he may live. Yet I myself have not been called to go in to the king these thirty days."

Trusting in the Lord to help his people, Mordecai sent word back to the queen: "Do not think in your heart that you will escape in the king's palace any more than all the other Jews. For if you remain completely silent at this time, relief and deliverance will arise for the Jews from another place, but you and your father's house will perish. Yet who knows whether you have come to the kingdom for such a time as this?"

When Esther received this challenge, she sent instructions to Mordecai: "Go, gather all the Jews who are present in Shushan, and fast for me; neither eat nor drink for three days, night or day. My maids and I will fast likewise. And so I will go to the king, which is against the law; and if I perish, I perish!"

Mordecai did as the queen asked. On the third day Esther put on her royal robes and went to the inner courtyard of the king's house. King Xerxes, seated on his throne, saw the queen standing outside. He held out his golden scepter, and Esther came near and touched it.

> **GOD SAYS:**
> " 'Yet who knows whether you have come to the kingdom for such a time as this?' " -Esther 4:14

"What do you wish, Queen Esther?" asked the king. "What is your request? It shall be given to you—up to half the kingdom!"

"If it pleases the king, let the king and Haman come today

to the banquet that I have prepared for him."

So the king and Haman went to the banquet that Esther had prepared. King Xerxes pressed her again about what she wanted. "What is your petition?" he asked. "It shall be granted you. What is your request, up to half the kingdom? It shall be done!"

The queen replied softly, "My petition and request is this: If I have found favor in the sight of the king, and if it pleases the king to grant my petition and fulfill my request, then let the king and Haman come to the banquet which I will prepare for them, and tomorrow I will do as the king has said."

Haman was so happy to be the special guest of the queen that he rushed home to tell his wife. "Queen Esther invited no one but me to come in with the king to the banquet that she prepared," he said proudly. "And tomorrow I am again invited by her, along with the king. Yet all this avails me nothing, so long as I see Mordecai the Jew sitting at the king's gate," he finished with a frown.

Haman's wife and his friends proposed that a high gallows be built. They suggested that in the morning he ask the king for permission to hang Mordecai. Haman liked the idea, and he had the gallows erected at once.

That night the king could not sleep. To help him pass the hours he had a scribe bring the records of the kingdom and read them to him. Soon the scribe came to the account of how Mordecai caught the two traitors who had planned to kill the king.

"What honor or dignity has been bestowed on Mordecai for this?" Xerxes asked.

His servants replied, "Nothing has been done for him."

By this time it was early morning. "Who is in the court?" the king wanted to know.

Now Haman had gotten up very early that morning and had come into the palace to request that the king hang Mordecai. One of the king's servants noticed him and announced, "Haman is there, standing in the court."

"Let him come in," said the king.

So Haman approached, and the king asked him, "What shall be done for the man whom the king delights to honor?"

Haman thought to himself, *Whom would the king delight to honor more than me?* So, the proud man said, "For the man whom the king delights to honor, let a royal robe be brought which the king has worn, and a horse on which the king has ridden, which has a royal crest placed on its head. Then let this robe and horse be delivered to the hand of one of the king's most noble princes, that he may array the man whom the king delights to honor. Then parade him on horseback through the city square, and proclaim before him: 'Thus shall it be done to the man whom the king delights to honor!' "

"Hurry," the king said to Haman, "take the robe and the horse, as you have suggested, and do so for Mordecai the Jew who sits within the king's gate! Leave nothing undone of all that you have spoken."

THOUGHT QUESTION:
Why did Esther wait three days before going into the king?

Haman didn't know what to say! He couldn't believe his ears. But he knew he would be executed if he didn't obey. So, Haman took the robe and the horse, put the robe on Mordecai, and led him on horseback through the city square, shouting, "Thus shall it be done to the man whom the king delights to honor!"

Afterward, Mordecai returned to his post at the king's gate. Haman rushed home weeping and with his head covered. However, instead of comforting her husband, Haman's wife gave him a warning. She saw the danger Haman was in and said, "If Mordecai, before whom you have begun to fall, is of Jewish descent, you will not prevail against him but will surely fall before him."

While Haman and his wife were still talking, the king's servants arrived to take him to Queen Esther's second banquet. As the king and Haman dined with her, King Xerxes asked again,

"What is your petition, Queen Esther? It shall be granted you. And what is your request, up to half the kingdom? It shall be done!"

"If I have found favor in your sight, O king," Esther answered, "and if it pleases the king, let my life be given me at my petition, and my people at my request. For we have been sold, my people and I, to be destroyed, to be killed, and to be annihilated."

"Who is he, and where is he, who would dare presume in his heart to do such a thing?" demanded the king.

"The adversary and enemy is this wicked Haman!" exclaimed Esther, pointing to the chief prince.

King Xerxes stood up in great anger and stomped out into the palace garden. Haman was terrified. He stood before Queen Esther and begged for his life. When the king came back to the banquet room, Haman had fallen

QUICK FACT: In Persia, once the king made a law, it could not be changed.

across the couch where Esther was sitting. The king said, "Will he also assault the queen while I am in the house?"

As he said this, his servants covered Haman's face. They knew that he was already condemned to death. One of the eunuchs said to the king, "Look! The gallows, fifty cubits high, which Haman made for Mordecai, who spoke good on the king's behalf, is standing at the house of Haman."

"Hang him on it!" the king ordered.

After Haman was hanged on his own gallows, the anger of Xerxes began to subside.

Then King Xerxes called a scribe to write a message for the Jews in all the provinces. Special messengers rode swiftly with the message to all parts of the empire, telling the Jews to gather in groups and fight for their lives on the day that had been set for their destruction. The Jews gathered in armed bands and defended themselves and their families on that day. The following day the Jews celebrated and held feasts. Queen Esther issued a proclamation that the Jews should keep that day annually as a day of feasting and joy.

THE RETURN TO JERUSALEM

Ezra 1–10; Nehemiah 1–13

Y ou'll remember that when King Nebuchadnezzar attacked Judah, he burned the city of Jerusalem and destroyed Solomon's temple. He took the people of Judah as captives to Babylon. Because they had disobeyed the Lord and worshiped idols, God allowed them to fall into the hands of their enemies.

For years the Jews lived in exile in Babylon, but they never forgot their homeland. After years of captivity, the people of Judah came to realize what it meant to be without a temple. They missed having a place where they could worship God and offer sacrifices, and they determined never to worship idols again. They wept when they thought of the ruins of the once glorious city of Jerusalem.

When the army of Cyrus surrounded Babylon during the reign of Belshazzar, the captives began to have hope. They knew the prophecy written by Isaiah more than a hundred years before the birth of Cyrus. The prophecy said that Cyrus would be the man to free the exiles and help them return home. With happiness they read these words again:

"Thus says the Lord to His anointed,
To Cyrus, whose right hand I have held—
To subdue nations before him
And loose the armor of kings,
To open before him the double doors,
So that the gates will not be shut:
'I will go before you
And make the crooked places straight;
I will break in pieces the gates of bronze
And cut the bars of iron.
I will give you the treasures of darkness
And hidden riches of secret places,
That you may know that I, the Lord,
Who call you by your name,
Am the God of Israel' " (Isaiah 45:1–3).

The Lord had also told Isaiah that Cyrus would rebuild Jerusalem. This prophecy came to pass in the first year of the reign of Cyrus the Persian, when he made the following decree:

"All the kingdoms of the earth the Lord God of heaven has given me. And He has commanded me to build Him a house at Jerusalem which is in Judah. Who is among you of all His people? May his God be with him, and let him go up to Jerusalem which is in Judah, and build the

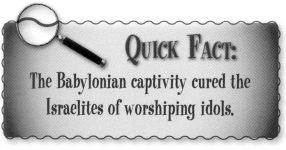

QUICK FACT:
The Babylonian captivity cured the Israelites of worshiping idols.

house of the Lord God of Israel (He is God), which is in Jerusalem. And whoever is left in any place where he dwells, let the men of his place help him with silver and gold, with goods and livestock, besides the freewill offerings for the house of God which is in Jerusalem."

None of the Jews were forced to return to the land of Canaan. Families could choose to go or stay as they wished. Zerubbabel, a descendant of King David, was placed in charge of the returning caravan, and the high priest Jeshua went with him.

About forty-two thousand people chose to go back to Judah. With all their servants and animals, they were a vast caravan as they crossed the hot and dreary desert. When the people arrived in their country, they spread out and went to the cities they had lived in before.

Seven months later, all of the people gathered in Jerusalem. Jeshua and the priests, along with Zerubbabel and his brothers, built an altar to God. From that day on, daily sacrifices were offered as God had commanded. The people again kept the Feast of Tabernacles and other holy days. They brought offerings to Jerusalem for the purchase of building materials. Workmen made preparations to rebuild the temple.

Many of the great stones that had been the foundation of Solomon's temple were still lying in the rubble of the ruined city. Masons took these stones and prepared them for use in the new temple. A day came when they were ready to lay the cornerstone of the temple. The people in Jerusalem sang and shouted their happiness.

While work on the temple and the city walls was going on, evil men from Samaria came and tried to halt the project. Work stopped for a time, but with the help of the Persian king, the temple was finally completed. However, the walls and houses of the city continued to lie in ruins for many years.

THOUGHT QUESTION:

Why was it so important to the Israelites to rebuild the temple?

Artaxerxes was now the king of Persia. In his court, a Jew named Nehemiah was the king's cupbearer. This servant had to taste every drink offered to the king to prove that it was not poisoned. While Nehemiah was working at the court in Shushan, he began to pray and fast, asking the God of heaven to help his people restore the kingdom of Judah.

One day King Artaxerxes saw a troubled look on his servant Nehemiah's face and asked, "Why is your face sad, since you are not sick? This is nothing but sorrow of heart."

Nehemiah was afraid because the king had noticed his sadness. "May the king live forever!" Nehemiah said. "Why should my face not be sad, when the city, the place of my fathers' tombs, lies waste, and its gates are burned with fire?"

"What do you request?" the king asked.

Nehemiah prayed to God at that moment, and then said, "If it

> ## GOD SAYS:
> " 'The God of heaven Himself will prosper us; therefore we His servants will arise and build.' " –Nehemiah 2:20

pleases the king, and if your servant has found favor in your sight, I ask that you send me to Judah, to the city of my fathers' tombs, that I may rebuild it."

The king honored Nehemiah's request and sent him to Jerusalem with an escort of soldiers. Nehemiah carried with him letters to the governors of the provinces he would pass through on his long trip. He also carried gifts to help pay the cost of rebuilding the city.

After the king's cupbearer had been in Jerusalem for three days, he decided to survey the state of the rebuilding work. He got up in the middle of the night, called together a few men to accompany him, and rode his horse to look at the city walls. As he passed the gates into the city that had been burned down, he found lots of broken-down walls and ruined buildings. He had not yet told anyone in the city why he had come back.

The next morning Nehemiah gathered the leaders, priests, and officials together and said, "You see the distress that we are in, how Jerusalem lies waste, and its gates are burned with fire. Come and let us build the wall of Jerusalem, that we may no longer be a reproach." Then he told them about the goodness of King Artaxerxes and the help he had been promised.

Nehemiah organized the construction work. Under his direction, different groups of men took responsibility for sections of the wall. Even though the enemies of Judah came back and mocked them and tried to get in the way, the wall of Jerusalem was soon completely rebuilt. The people of Judah were settled once more in their little kingdom. They built a second temple, which was not as beautiful as Solomon's had been, since many of the treasures were still in Persia. The Most Holy Place was empty. The golden ark containing the Ten Commandments on tablets of stone had been hidden by Jeremiah when the city was about to be captured. It was never found again.

A NATION
RESTORED

Many families from the tribes of Judah and Benjamin returned to Jerusalem. However, thousands of Jews remained in Persia and Egypt after they were released from bondage. In these lands they became successful in business.

The people who returned to Jerusalem no longer worshiped idols. They loved the true God and served Him with complete loyalty. Jerusalem once more became a great center as Jews came from their homes in distant lands to worship God in the new temple.

As long as the Persians ruled the world, the people of Judah were safe from invasion. However, a new world empire came into being in 331 B.C. After a long war, Alexander the Great had defeated the Persians, and Greece became the new superpower. Soon the Greek army marched south to capture Jerusalem. Alexander had decided to punish the Jews for siding with Persia in the war.

When Alexander's army approached the city, Jaddua the high priest and all the temple priests marched out through the gates in solemn procession to meet the victorious leader. When the Jews surrendered to the Greek army, Alexander was so impressed with their dignity and honesty that he saluted the high priest. Thousands of people saw the kind act of the general, and they shouted with happiness. Alexander and Jaddua entered Jerusalem together, and Alexander offered sacrifices in the temple. The Greek leader gave the nation many freedoms, and Judah was secure until Alexander the Great died.

In 170 B.C., Antiochus Epiphanes came to the throne of Greece. He was determined to force the Jews to accept the pagan Greek religion and to worship idols. After conquering Egypt, Antiochus led his army to Jerusalem, broke down the walls, massacred thousands of Jews, and burned much of the city. He robbed the holy temple of its golden furniture and made a mockery of the worship of the Lord.

The Jews were forbidden to offer sacrifices, and they were not allowed to keep the Sabbath. Nevertheless, thousands of faithful men and women stood firm and refused to disobey the commandments of the Lord, preferring to die rather than sin against God.

When officers of Antiochus tried to enforce the emperor's orders, they were opposed by Mattathias, a priest of the temple. His five sons stood with their father, determined to gain freedom for their nation at any cost. When the enemy soldiers came to the high priest and offered him riches and honor if he would renounce his allegiance to God, Mattathias said that if all the heathen in the king's

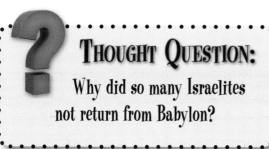

THOUGHT QUESTION:

Why did so many Israelites not return from Babylon?

dominions listen to him and forsake each of them the religion of his forefathers, and choose to follow his commands instead, yet I and my sons and my brothers will live in accordance with the agreement of our forefathers. God forbid that we should abandon the law and the ordinances.

When he stopped speaking, a Jew stepped forward to offer a sacrifice to a Greek idol.

QUICK FACT: The Israelites now followed all God's laws carefully. They had finally learned their lesson.

Mattathias sprang forward and killed the man. In the fight that followed, he also killed the chief officer of Antiochus. This started a fierce revolution, led by a son of Mattathias, Judas Maccabaeus.

After the time of Antiochus, the Romans became rulers of the world. In 63 B.C., the Roman general Pompey captured Jerusalem. Many faithful Jews were killed defending the city and the temple. But Pompey did not plunder the Holy Place or take away any of its treasures.

While the Roman governor Herod the Great ruled Judea, he tried to gain the favor of the Jews by rebuilding the ruined temple. He was an evil, ambitious ruler, and many of the Jews hated him. It was during his reign that Jesus, the Son of Mary, was born in Bethlehem.

For hundreds of years the Jewish nation had looked for the coming of the promised Messiah. For hundreds of years they had read the prophecies concerning the mighty Deliverer who would save His people. The little town of Bethlehem, where David grew up, was to be the birthplace of the Messiah. Micah, the prophet of God, had said:

"But you, Bethlehem Ephrathah,
Though you are little among the thousands of Judah,
Yet out of you shall come forth to Me
The One to be Ruler in Israel,
Whose goings forth are from of old,
From everlasting" (Micah 5:2).

GOD SAYS:
" 'Behold, the virgin shall be with child, and bear a Son, and they shall call His name Immanuel.' "
-Matthew 1:23

All of Judah was waiting for the coming of the Son of God, the Mighty Prince, who would save His people from their sins.